D0801792

THE

CAPTAIN JACK SPARROW

🕱 HANDBOOK 🕱

THE

CAPTAIN JACK SPARROW

💀 HANDBOOK 💀

A SWASHBUCKLER'S GUIDE
FROM THE
PIRATES OF THE CARIBBEAN

By Jason Heller

QUIRK BOOKS
PHILADELPHIA

AHOY, ALL YE WOULD-BE PIRATES, TAKE HEED: This book is a work of entertainment. The publisher and author hereby disclaim any liability from an injury that may result from the use, proper or improper, of the information contained in this book. We do not guarantee that this information is safe, complete, or wholly accurate, nor should it be considered a substitute for a reader's good judgment and common sense.

Copyright © 2011 by Disney Enterprises, Inc.
All rights reserved. No part of this book may be reproduced in any form
without written permission from the publisher.
Library of Congress Cataloging in Publication Number: 2010941019
ISBN: 978-1-59474-504-1
Printed in Singapore

Typeset in Bembo, Blackmoor, Dear Sarah
Design by Doogie Horner
Illustrations by Eugene Smith
Production management by John J. McGurk

Quirk Books
215 Church Street
Philadelphia, PA 19106
www.quirkbooks.com

10 9 8 7 6 5 4 3 2 1

CONTENTS

CHAPTER THREE: PEOPLE SKILLS

CHAPTER FOUR: ACQUIRING BOOTY

CHAPTER FIVE: CHEATING DEATH

CHAPTER SIX: MYSTERIES OF THE DEEP

APPENDIX: PIRATICAL LINGO

"Wherever we want to go, we'll go. That's what a ship is, you know. It's not just a keel and a hull and a deck and sails. That's what a ship needs, but what a ship is—what the Black Pearl really is—is freedom."

—CAPTAIN JACK SPARROW

Introduction

P IRATES, BY NATURE, AREN'T TERRIBLY LITERATE. AS A CONSE-QUENCE, NO BOOK CAN HOPE TO FULLY PREPARE THE PAMPERED, MODERN-DAY LAYABOUT FOR THE LUSTY LIFE OF A PIRATE.

This book, however, will put you on the right path—the path to adventure, treasure, glory, mystery, and, every so often, the bottom of a barrel of rum.

In a day and age when piracy is associated more with downloading than swashbuckling, the need for the free, roguish life of a pirate has never been greater. The only problem is finding a suitable role model. Surely there is none living, but since the Golden Age of Piracy of the eighteenth century, one name has echoed throughout the ages: that scourge of the Caribbean, Captain Jack Sparrow.

Sparrow was no teacher, but he was a thinker. In fact, his wits saved him from certain doom more often than did sheer brute force, and therein lies the foremost lesson *The Captain Jack Sparrow Handbook* aims to impart. Caught up in the roar of the ocean and the ring of clashed swords, far too many pirates of the golden age succumbed to the stereotype of the artless, primitive brigand (not to mention succumbing to hangmen, sea monsters, and the devilish Davy Jones). A cutlass and a musketoon, as any successful scoundrel knows, can get you only so far. When it comes to the craft of piracy, subtlety is far more effective.

In this book, you'll be given a parrot's-eye view of the pirate's trade, including tips on sailing a ship, liberating treasure, captaining a crew, dealing with magic, distinguishing different kinds of pirates, and disarming an enemy with words alone. When all else fails, there's always running. Running is good.

Never forget, though, that nothing could be less worthy of a true pirate than snooty scholarship. As Sparrow once famously said, "The only rules that really matter are these: what a man can do and what a man can't do." Accordingly, this book shouldn't be considered gold-plated law or gospel truth, but rather a fast-and-loose list of amenable suggestions—"more what you'd call guidelines than actual rules," to quote Sparrow's notorious associate, the blackguard Hector Barbossa.

Piracy, after all, is about making your own way in the world. At the occasional expense of those more fortunate than yourself, of course.

CHAPTER ONE

PIRACY 101

The first step toward soliciting membership in the august brotherhood of pirates is asking yourself: Do I really want to do this?

In case the misadventures of Captain Jack Sparrow weren't enough to warn you away from life on the high seas, it bears repeating that a pirate's life is fraught with peril, hardship, poor hygiene, and some really bad food. On the upside, you get to be a pirate: feared, loathed, whispered about, envied, and, above all, as free as an albatross on a gulf breeze.

Once you're secure in your conviction, keep the following tips in mind. They might save you years of frustration—or, at the very least, spare you a sordid initiation.

How to Become a Pirate

WELL, YOU'VE GOT TO START SOMEWHERE. AND YOU CAN'T START RIGHT OUT AS A CAPTAIN, BECAUSE YOU'VE GOT TO EARN THAT LOFTY STATUS—WHETHER FAIRLY OR OTHER-WISE. SO LET'S BEGIN WITH THE BASICS.

If you're going to be a pirate, you need to look like a pirate, sound like a pirate, keep up with the pirates, and be accepted by the pirates. Sure, you want to be a colorful individual with a fearsome reputation. But as with most social groups, you'll need to first fit in well enough to be accepted before you can deviate enough to be admired. Which is to say: Impress them at the job interview first, and impress them with surprises once you've got the gig.

The following four steps are the fundamentals for any would-be pirate.

1. MAKE SURE YOU CAN SWIM. Believe it or not, many a would-be pirate has wound up feeding sharks at the bottom of the Jamaica Channel. With, you know, their own flesh. Walking the plank or swimming to shore is an everyday occupational hazard—not to mention saving drowning damsels—so swimming should be as easy and natural to you as skipping through a meadow. (Not that pirates skip through meadows, mind you.)

   If it's been a while since you've taken a dip in the salty deep, proceed immediately to the nearest beach and start practicing your breaststroke, backstroke, forward crawl, and dog paddle—not to mention holding your breath, a skill pirates are called on to exercise often and without warning. If you live in a landlocked area, the pool of your local recreation center will do for a dip. But if you want to be a sea dog, shouldn't you start thinking about moving someplace with a sea? Just a thought.

2. DRESS LIKE A PIRATE. Despite the apparent anachronism, your town's annual Renaissance Faire is an ideal place to shop for pirate garb. After all, the Golden Age of Piracy begins almost exactly where the Renaissance ends—that is, roughly around 1700—and pirates prided themselves on wearing castoffs and slightly outdated clothing. They were, in a sense, the punk rockers of their time—Jack Sparrow more so than others. In any case, the faire should offer a wide array of suitable pants, shirts, doublets, jerkins, vests, belts, and hats. Pay particular attention to the hat. A pirate's hat, invariably of the tricorne or three-cornered style, is a symbol of his stature, his pride, and his sartorial panache.

Of course, female pirates like Angelica usually wear men's clothing, more for convenience than anything else—although some did impersonate men outright, which is a wholly acceptable practice (see "How to Disguise Your Gender," page 77). That said, it's also perfectly fine for a female pirate to flaunt her femininity in any way she sees fit, including the wearing of skirts, dresses, and bodices.

A word of wisdom to the beginner: Despite the romance surrounding such clichéd accoutrements as peg legs and eye patches, they aren't all they're cracked up to be. Restricting vision in one eye inhibits your depth perception, which can be crucial in matters of naval maintenance and navigation (see "Maritime Skills," page 36). As for wooden legs, well, you need to be missing a *real* leg before you can wear one. We don't recommend being in too much of a hurry to do that. There are, after all, plenty of men and monsters of the sea willing to oblige you.

3.   COME UP WITH A PIRATE NAME. Like rock stars or criminals, pirates love using aliases. Which makes sense, seeing as how pirates *are*, in a way, both rock stars and criminals. Not all pirate aliases are fanciful, however. In most cases, it's better to choose a nondescript name, something that doesn't detract from your image—that is, the one you'll be building and exaggerating (see "How to Spin Your Own Myth," page 81). Names as mundane as Charles, Anne, and, of course, Jack have worked well for many pirates. You just want to make sure that authorities can't track down your family or friends, all of whom would probably be more than happy to turn you in—especially if the reward is right.

You also don't want to call yourself something cartoonish or boastful, like Plundering Bob or Slash-and-Sink Kate, seeing as how that will get you laughed out of the pirate community faster than you can scupper a dinghy. Granted, some of the most luminary pirates in history, like Blackbeard, Edward England, and Calico Jack, have used colorful aliases, but it's not recommended for the novice. Drawing too much attention to yourself is a bad idea, at least until you're better accustomed to dodging blockades and musket balls.

4.   SIGN ON TO A PIRATE CREW. Some people are lucky enough to wake up after a drunken night in a seaside tavern to find themselves press-ganged into a pirate crew, stuck on a ship sailing halfway to Barbados.

Sadly, such good fortune can't be counted on. After picking a name, dressing the part, and shoring up your swimming skills, it's time to track down a recruiter.

Recruiters can usually be found in the seediest watering hole closest to the docks. For his recruiting, Jack Sparrow often used the grimy tavern known as the Faithful Bride, on the Haitian island of Tortuga. Look for a line made up of the most tattered, shambling, sorry excuses for seafarers you can find—a line with, at its head, a smiling man holding out a quill and a contract—and queue up.

But be warned: Although it's customary, and forward-thinking, for pirate captains to distribute all loot equally among crew members, they also lie outrageously about the length of service and threshold of danger for a particular voyage. Yet, when starting out as a pirate, you can't be too picky. Just swallow the recruiting spiel, close your eyes, and sign on the dotted line. After all, it's only an alias you're putting down in ink.

How to Recognize a Fellow Pirate

N O PIRATE IS AN ISLAND. ONCE YOU'VE FIRMLY DECIDED TO BE-COME A BRIGAND OF THE HIGH SEAS, YOU'LL NATURALLY GRAVITATE TOWARD YOUR OWN KIND. BUT BEFORE EVEN THINKING OF ENLISTING SHIPMATES OF YOUR OWN (SEE "HOW TO RECRUIT A CREW," PAGE 60), YOU NEED TO FIND OTHER PIRATES—AND THEY DON'T EXACTLY ADVERTISE OPENLY. PICKING UP ON THE SUBTLE, TELL-TALE TRAITS OF A SURREPTITIOUS PIRATE IS THE BEST WAY TO MAKE NEW

FRIENDS. HERE ARE A FEW DEAD GIVEAWAYS EVEN THE MOST COVERTLY DISGUISED PIRATE CAN'T HELP BUT DROP.

1. THE WALK. Today we often refer to criminals taking the "walk of shame." In the heyday of the sea pirate, there was no such thing. Those who showed weakness or hesitation on the wharves of the Caribbean were easy pickings for pickpockets and press-gangers; the savvy pirate, therefore, is one who struts boldly and colorfully. Jack Sparrow is the master of this stride: His extravagant, boldly unsteady step has been known to intimidate and confound just as effectively as does his sword. The trick in looking for such a person is tuning your senses to home in on the small, peculiar differences in gait that separate a pirate from, say, some poor sot who's merely missing a few toes (or wits).

    With practice and a sharp eye, you can begin to discern in pirates a complex and at times gravity-defying pattern of ambulation: The natural rolling, side-to-side gait of the perennially seaborne—which comes from the pitch of a ship upon the waves—is augmented on land by an understated yet profound swagger that subliminally sends the signal to any potential predator: "There's a tiger shark lurking beneath this landlubber garb."

    Of course, other (less complimentary) influences are at play in a pirate's sly strut—namely, the nimble navigation of a springy plank tiptoed at musket-point and the extravagant lope of the habitually rum-sodden. But there's no need to boast of such things among polite company.

2.   THE TALK. The argot of the pirate is a complex one. In essence, the pirate language is a pidgin of the slangs of seafarers throughout the ages, including the corsairs of the Mediterranean, the picaroons of England, and the natives of the Caribbean isles.

That's not to say that the salty accent of the pirate—and particularly of Jack Sparrow, who possesses a rum-infused speech entirely his own—is something unintelligible to the layman or lubber; rather, its close kinship to the King's English means that pirates aren't instantly recognizable by their speech alone. Which is as it should be. As with pirate walking, pirate talking should be a subtle variation on what's socially acceptable. Littering one's diction with the blasphemy of your average buccaneer is far less desirable than lightly dropped, thinly veiled references to hearties, jolliness, and the letter X (see Piratical Lingo, page 167).

Also, despite far too many popular (and, frankly, demeaning) depictions, self-respecting pirates don't punctuate their speech with nonsense like "Arrrr!" Unless, of course, they're cleverly impersonating someone *impersonating* a pirate, in which case such poor taste is in the service of a higher and hopefully profitable purpose (see "How to Use Words to Misdirect and Confound," page 72). Mind you, many pirates aren't self-respecting whatsoever, in which case "Arrrr!" is only natural.

3.   THE SMELL. This subject isn't pleasant enough to dwell on for long, so suffice it to say that pirates are a fragrant lot. Even Sparrow, that most dapper and charismatic of scoundrels, was given to a certain odiferous aura. Granted, all sailors are at least a little frightful when sensed from down-

wind, but pirates possess even less discipline than the average merchant or military man (see "Pirate Hygiene [or the Lack Thereof]," page 84).

Even when pirates do try to clean up, which is seldom, the compounded perfume of fish, tar, and soiled laundry tends to cling to them like a bad memory. When all else fails in your search for a fellow pirate, follow your nose.

4. THE TATTOOS. The origins of tattooing are ancient and unknowable, but one thing seems likely: Pirates were responsible for introducing them to Western culture. At the very least, they gave tattoos their menacing, outlaw reputation, one that persists in part to this day. Sailors of reputable vessels once used telescopes to scour the decks of oncoming ships, looking for a telltale tattoo that would identify the crew as pirates.

   If sailors can do it, so can you. Keeping an eye out for tattoos, especially those peeking out from under sleeves at the forearm (such as Jack Sparrow's infamous mark showing his avian namesake, adjacent to a brand cruelly given to him by the East India Company) is an ideal way to identify a potential pirate. The designs are often unimaginative and predictable: skulls, skeletons, ships, and even the occasional favorite strumpet.

   Sparrow, of course, is known for a most unorthodox tattoo—a poetic text—across his back. However, you might not get a chance to see such dazzling inkwork unless a pirate is being flogged in public—which, to be precise, is not exactly rare for a pirate.

5. THE BRETHREN COURT. After you've established some sort of contact with a fellow pirate—hopefully one that doesn't involve side-by-

side sentences in the stockade—the next step is to seek out the Brethren Court. Also known as the Order of the Brethren, the Pirate Council, and Brethren of the Coast, this secret society of brigands and blackguards is widely reported to have been abolished toward the end of the seventeenth century. But who do you think spread such rumors? The Court is furtive and unfathomable, and membership can mean access to the accumulated wisdom of centuries of piratehood.

So how does one recognize a member of the Brethren Court? Don't even think about it. There is no secret handshake or card, and only nine Pirate Lords may serve at any one time. They are known by the pieces of eight they carry as well as by the shanty "Hoist the Colours," which they sing to call a conclave to order. If you're fortunate and perceptive enough to follow such clues, the best you can do is try to offer your services as a subservient. Serving on the crew of a Pirate Lord is the only way to fast-track your pirate career (and, if you're extremely loyal and trustworthy, become a Lord yourself one day).

Lastly, don't make the mistake of taking the word *brethren* to mean "male only." Not only do lady pirates abound throughout the history of the Court, the legendary Elizabeth Swann became one of the greatest pirates in history. Pirates may be a loutish lot, but talent is talent, regardless of the package in which it is wrapped (see "How to Disguise Your Gender," page 77).

How to Pass the Time

A S STATED EARLIER, PIRATES ARE NOT, BY AND LARGE, MEN AND WOMEN OF LETTERS. EVEN JACK SPARROW IS A MAN RULED MORE BY NATURAL, SEA-SHARPENED WIT THAN BY A HEAD STUFFED FULL OF DUSTY, BOOK-BOUND IDEAS. AS LOW AS PIRATE LITER-ACY IS, THOUGH, A FEW ACCIDENTALLY EDUCATED ROGUES DO FIGURE AMONG THEIR RANKS—THOUGH THESE COVERT INTELLECTUALS ARE CAREFUL NOT TO BE CAUGHT READING BOOKS OR KEEPING JOURNALS WHILE AT SEA. AFTER ALL, NOTHING IS LESS DIGNIFIED THAN AN OTHER-WISE LUSTY PIRATE WITH HIS OR HER NOSE STUCK IN A BOOK. (NEEDLESS TO SAY, NEVER BRAG ABOUT HAVING READ THIS ONE.) STILL, THERE ARE PLENTY OF FAR MORE APPROPRIATE PASTIMES TO HELP CONSUME THOSE LONG STRETCHES OF BOREDOM BETWEEN LOOTING AND PILLAGING.

1. PICK A PET. When the royal courts of Europe began to establish menageries, the forerunners to modern zoos, the demand for exotic animals from the New World increased dramatically. Exotic birds like parrots became not only valuable commodities but a kind of status symbol as well. In other words, a parrot on the shoulder is more or less a pirate's idea of bling. Talking bling, that is. The procurement of a parrot by illicit means is hardly worth the risk, however; a local pet store is safer. An added benefit of keeping a parrot: When a long voyage begins to addle one's brain, conversing with a parrot is a good way to talk to oneself without really talking to oneself.

    Parrots aren't the only animal companions that pirates have seen

MONKEYS: LESS CLICHÉD THAN PARROTS

fit to adopt. Dogs and cats have been seen aboard many a pirate vessel. Cats, especially polydactyl (extra-toed) ones, are much-needed
mousers and they're considered good luck on a ship (see "Top Ten
Pirate Superstitions," page 158). The most useful pet of all, however,
is the monkey. Not only can these little creatures be trained to fetch
items and distract enemies, but, by dint of their comedic shenanigans,
they can lighten the dreary, day-to-day toil of sailing. (One such
notable simian sidekick is Jack, Captain Hector Barbossa's famed
capuchin monkey named in jest after Jack Sparrow.) Yes, even the
most bloodthirsty pirate needs a good laugh now and again.

2.   MAKE MUSIC. Musicmaking has always been a primal urge of humans—and pirates, as inhuman as they can sometimes be, are no different. The *Black Pearl*, even at its most cursed, was known to ring with
the joyously tuneless cacophony of pirate song. The single-reed instrument known as the hornpipe is a particular favorite, as are simple
drums, whether professionally crafted or jury-rigged from whatever is
lying around the cabin. But a pirate's first and foremost instrument of
choice is his voice. In many ways, singing is part and parcel of piracy. It
gives crewmates a chance to boast, tell stories, commiserate, and cele-
brate the life of freedom that only a pirate can know. Many pirate songs
or sea shanties have arisen over the centuries, including "Dead Man's
Chest," its well-known spinoff "Yo Ho (A Pirate's Life for Me)," and
the ceremonial "Hoist the Colours," the anthem of the Brethren Court.
Knowing all the lyrics, singing in key, and/or having any natural mu-
sical ability are all minor considerations. What are the rules of music,
after all, but just more laws to flaunt?

Yet, for a pirate, music isn't all fun and games. It has a practical aspect as well: The macabre, sing-along dance known as capering—mixed with the rhythmic blowing of horns and beating of drums known as vaporing—together form a pirate's first line of offense. After firing a warning shot across the bow of an intended victim's ship, a pirate crew will caper and vapor within sight of the targeted vessel, with the intent of intimidating them into quick and easy surrender. Despite their fearsome reputation, pirates avoid violence as often as possible, relying more on bluffs, threats, and psychological warfare. And few things are as psychologically warlike as a gang of pirates trying to sing and dance. Especially if, by the light of the moon, said pirates are made entirely of bones, as was the crew of the *Black Pearl* under Captain Barbossa.

3. EAT (BUT TRY NOT TO DRINK) UP. The word *buccaneer* has become synonymous with *pirate*, but it once had a far different definition, referring to French hunters in the Caribbean known for their smoked meats. In other words, food and piracy are inextricably linked, which is odd, seeing as how culinary expertise is hardly a hallmark of the pirate. The sea-kettle of the ship's cook is one of the most neglected parts of a pirate ship—and that's really saying something—although pirates, like all people, love a good meal. Surprisingly, seafood does not rank high in their menu, mostly because pirates are poor fishermen (mostly be choice, seeing as how the mundane task of throwing a line into the ocean seems undignified to even the lowliest of their ilk, accustomed as they are to taking what they want by force).

Ironically, land-farmed meat, such as poultry and pork, is far more favorable to your average pirate, and a ship is usually stocked with these types of victuals each time it's docked. The lack of refrigeration, however, is a problem, usually solved by salting and curing or simply turning the most dubious cuts into some form of stew. The common, dried, tooth-breaking sailor bread known as hardtack is laughed at by any self-respecting scourge of the sea. And scurvy, the bane of all sea-goers, presents only a minor concern to pirates operating among the subtropical isles of the Caribbean, where vitamin-rich fruits (avocado, tamarind, mango, papaya) are ripe for the picking.

Another ostensible staple of the pirate diet—alcohol—is not as widespread as popular stereotypes would have you believe. A drunk pirate is a dead pirate, after all, since an outlaw can only survive by keeping his wits about him at all times. (The legendary Welsh priva-teer Henry Morgan is said to have died from liver failure due to alcoholism, which is hardly a fitting way for a warrior to go.) That's not to say that pirates don't willfully perpetuate and capitalize on the image of the brandy-bathed, grog-gargling, rum-muddled marauder. After all, when trying to outfox one's enemies, *acting* drunk is better than *being* drunk.

TYPES OF PIRATES

BUCCANEER: Now synonymous with the word *pirate* (at least in the Caribbean), *buccaneer* is a term originally applied to game hunters on the shores of Hispaniola. It was adopted by the French from the Indian word *bukan,* the distant ancestor of today's *barbecue.* Buccaneers aren't above lighting a few fires themselves in their quest for loot, mayhem, and glory.

CORSAIR: The term *corsair* can be applied to both French privateers and Islamic ones—the latter having marauded across the Mediterranean from the Muslim nations of North Africa, attacking Christian ships. Both sets of corsairs were populated with a range of sea-rovers, from villainous to valiant. Lord Byron immortalized the corsair in his epic poem of the same name.

PRIVATEER: Although many pirates were once military men, privateers were more often ranking naval officers given license—in the form of letters of marquee granted by a monarch—to legally plunder the ships of that nation's enemies. That didn't make them any less blood-thirsty, however, nor did it mean they gave up their plundering ways after the commission had ended. The term could also be used as a slight insult between pirates (see "Pirate Insults," page 86).

PIRATE: In what we'd like to think of as a bit of linguistic hijacking, the word *pirate* has more or less overtaken all other names for the sorts of scourges and scalawags we all know and love. Real-life pirates exist today—including despicable violent brigands as well as gentler pillagers of the Internet—but the classic, swashbuckling lifestyle (minus the crime) is the kind of piracy truly worth idolizing. To a sensible degree, of course. Captain Jack Sparrow is perhaps the quintessential pirate, although his Brethren who hold him in enmity and envy might disagree.

PIRATE GARB AND GEAR

1. BANDANA
2. BELT
3. BELT BUCKLE
4. BOOTS
5. BRAIDS [HAIR]
6. DRAWERS
7. FROCK COAT

8. JEWELRY
9. POUCHES
10. SASH
11. SHIRT
12. TRICORNE HAT
13. VEST

1
12
5
7
8
11
9
13
2
3
10
6
4

PIRATE GARB AND GEAR

BLACKBEARD: THE
BLACK STANDARD

Of all the sea-rovers who ever hoisted the black colors, Blackbeard is the most notorious. And rightfully so. Ruthless, cunning, and savage to his subordinates, he was nonetheless an able and even charismatic leader. An Englishman who was born Edward Teach, he began his career of plunder as one of the many privateers dispensed by King George to raid enemy ships during war. It wasn't until he struck out as a free agent that his true legend was born.

Blackbeard and his zombie crew have become known for raising havoc throughout the Caribbean. It is said that Blackbeard wields a mystical weapon—the Sword of Triton—which he uses to control his ship, the *Queen Anne's Revenge.* His crew of ghastly zombies obey his every command, and they don't fear death because, well, they're already dead.

It's difficult to imagine that a woman could ever be attracted to a man who puts lit fuses in his beard (how would she kiss him without getting burnt?), but rumor has it that Blackbeard does indeed have offspring—a daughter named Angelica who loves him despite his morally corrupt lifestyle.

THE ~~FIVE~~ SIX OTHER GREATEST PIRATES

1. SIR HENRY MORGAN. Where Blackbeard was a demon, Sir Henry Morgan was a downright devil. Although the Welsh-born admiral and privateer deserves applause for solidifying the Brethren Court (see page 21), the methods by which he brought order and strengthened piracy in the Caribbean were atrocious. Torture and treachery were among his many and habitual transgressions. Although he was knighted and granted a lieutenant governorship of Jamaica, Morgan died of drunkenness, belligerent as ever, and sadly sealed the stereotype of the buccaneer as a subhuman lout. (Which, granted, is only a slight exaggeration, despite a pirate's many redeeming qualities.) Jack Sparrow is almost as well known for his own love of rum, but thankfully he's much more of a merry drunk.

2. BARTHOLOMEW "BLACK BART" ROBERTS. Though known for his dashing appearance—marked by a predilection for feathers, gold, diamonds, and a silk holster to hold his pistols—Bartholomew "Black Bart" Roberts was anything but a gentleman. He looted as many ships and took as many prisoners as any of his contemporaries, but he was also known for a certain paradoxical moderation; preferring tea over rum and discipline over chaos, he famously drafted the Pirate Code of Conduct. The code's eleven articles forbade women onboard, gambling, infighting, desertion, poor upkeep of weapons, and lights after dark aboard ship. They were also progressive in ensuring certain rights to members of a pirate crew, including a vote

ANNE BONNY, CALICO JACK, AND MARY READ

in the ship's affairs, disability insurance, an equal share of all booty, and—most colorfully—a guarantee of the availability of musicians at all times to maintain the crew's high spirits.

3. CALICO JACK RACKHAM. Unlike his contemporary Blackbeard, Calico Jack Rackham seemed to go out of his way to refrain from the typical barbarism of a pirate. His most noteworthy exploit involves returning a ship, intact and unharmed, to the unfortunate captain he had just robbed blind. In fact, this uncharacteristic restraint is Rackham's claim to fame; otherwise, he was a mostly small-time pirate who commanded a single, small sloop rather than an armada full of buccaneers. But that restraint is noteworthy. It shows that not every pirate has to be brutal for the sake of brutality—and that, as with most groups of people, pirates are often unfairly represented by their most dramatic, colorful, and controversial constituents. Rackham had another saving grace as well: He gave his lover Anne Bonney, destined to become one of the greatest woman pirates of all time, her first taste of the sea. Reports of a rivalry between Calico Jack and that other great pirate of the same first name, Jack Sparrow, are entirely unfounded—although it is easy to imagine a little friction between the two.

4. & 5. ANNE BONNY AND MARY READ. Black Bart's pirate code may have sought to forbid women from pirate ships, but that didn't stop untold numbers of female buccaneers from joining the ranks. The most celebrated of these femmes fatales are Anne Bonny and Mary Read. Bonney got her start as the kept woman of Calico Jack Rackham, but she wasn't a woman anyone could keep for long. After disguising herself as a man to join Rackham's crew, the incendiary Bonny became attracted to a fellow crewmember—only to find that her new "fellow" was Mary Read, *another* woman wearing breeches and passing herself off as a male pirate (see "How to Disguise Your Gender," page 77). A devoted friendship bloomed between the two women, who eventually achieved notoriety in a daring, two-woman, pistol-and-cutlass defense of the ship against English privateers. Not only were they two of the bravest pirates ever to swashbuckle, Bonny and Read showed that even relatively progressive pirates like Black Bart were bound by the prejudices of their time. It's hard to say whether the pair served as a personal inspiration to Angelica; it may well have been the other way around.

6. CAPTAIN JACK SPARROW. How Captain Jack Sparrow wriggled his way into the pantheon of great pirate captains and attained the rank of Pirate Lord, we'll never know. The fact remains, though, that his widely chronicled exploits have granted him a rather nefarious legend; taking cues from his incorrigible swagger and disarming charm certainly wouldn't hurt. Attempting to *repeat* his tragicomic misadventures would, of course, be insanity of the highest order. (Attempting to replicate his consumption of rum would be even crazier.)

A GREAT PIRATE—HE SAYS SO HIMSELF

CHAPTER TWO

MARITIME SKILLS

Casting off docking lines, gaining one's bearings, heading out to sea under the press of the mainsail: Sailing is one of humankind's noblest enterprises. But don't get all starry-eyed and romantic. It's also a dangerous, back-breaking method of transportation that any sane pirate views as a means to an end. Captain Jack Sparrow never learned more of the mariner's trade than absolutely necessary, which is probably why he regularly wound up sinking many small boats just as he was about to dock them. In this area, you don't want to be like him. Knowing the basics will help you become a valuable crew member. But remember: No matter how busy the activity on the deck, volunteer for nothing. If you wanted to work all day, you would not have become a pirate, now, would you? Still, you'll want to take the wheel from your helmsman from time to time, just to keep up appearances. So when circumstances force you to break a sweat onboard, make sure to take up a more specific and less complicated task than sailing the whole ship.

How to Climb Rigging

THERE'S A PRACTICAL REASON TO CLIMB A SHIP'S RIGGING—THAT IS, THE ROPES THAT HOLD THE MASTS IN PLACE. BUT HONESTLY, THAT'S BORING. AS A PIRATE, YOU'RE MOST CONCERNED WITH TAKING TO THE ROPES WHEN WAGING A BATTLE ONBOARD. THE ADVANTAGE IN A FIGHT ALWAYS GOES TO THE ONE ON HIGHER GROUND. AND SEEING AS HOW THERE'S NO GROUND AT SEA, THE RIGGING IS YOUR BEST ALTERNATIVE.

1. LOSE THE BOOTS. If you're wearing footwear—which many pirates choose to forgo while sailing—take them off. Men aren't monkeys, but we're close enough, and the added grip that comes from an unshod foot will help immensely as you scramble upward, pistol in sash and dagger in teeth. Jack Sparrow might not follow this rule, but he's experienced enough to get around it (and, in doing so, to keep his very fine boots). Remember, too, that the coarse ropes are coated with tar, which won't make you smell especially lovely but will help you stick to the job.

2. DON'T LOOK DOWN. The secret to climbing rigging is not to be afraid. The rope—usually stout hemp—that constitutes a ship's rigging may look slender, but it's astoundingly strong, crafted to withstand rotting caused by constant exposure to saltwater. Trust the rope. Be one with the rope. And fix your eyes skyward, venturing only cursory glances at the deck below. Maintaining faith in the integrity of the rigging and a willful ignorance of your true altitude will help you avoid panic and the effects of vertigo.

WRAP A ROPE AROUND WRIST FOR SAFETY

CLIMB BAREFOOT AND LOOK SKYWARD

3. GET INTO THE SWING OF IT. Often while a pirate is climbing rigging, someone less than friendly is following close behind. Swinging amid the rigging using loose lengths of rope not only helps you evade pursuers and defend your ship against potential boarders, it looks quite dashing as well. As soon as you've determined the highest point at which a rope is firmly attached, use cutlass or dagger to slice yourself a nice section to wrap around your wrist. The more firmly you do so, the less you need to worry about friction (or falling, which can be even more painful than an arm-long rope burn). Then simply aim for another stable-looking yardarm or web of rigging to land on, brace your shoulder, and push off. If you miss your landing, don't fret; you can either circle back in a wide arc to kick at an enemy in the ropes, or you can release the rope completely and go sailing into the drink—if, that is, you're within sight of land and feeling robust. If worse comes to worst, you can always use your knife another way: Stick the blade into sailcloth, hold firmly on the handle, and slide down as the knife slits the sail in half. Although, to be honest, the sheer insanity of such a move has made most pirates pause, and rightfully so.

How to Fire a Cannon

A S GALLANT AND GRANDIOSE AS HAND-TO-HAND COMBAT MAY APPEAR, TRUE PIRATES PREFER TO FIGHT FROM A DISTANCE. ACCORDINGLY, CANNONS ARE A TIME-HONORED PART OF THE NAUTICAL ARSENAL, ONE FAVORED PARTICULARLY BY THE BRETHREN (WHEN DEFENDING ONESELF AGAINST BEASTIES LIKE THE KRAKEN; SINKING A SHIP LOADED WITH BOTH BOOTY AND INNOCENT FOLK IS THE EPITOME OF FOOLHARDINESS). NEVERTHELESS, THE MAXIM HOLDS TRUE: THE BIGGER THE GUN, THE BIGGER THE BACKFIRE. CANNONS ARE NOT TO BE TRIFLED WITH, UNLESS YOU'RE LOOKING TO GET YOURSELF A PEG LEG. OR TWO.

1. BEWARE OF SPARKS. All it takes is one small spark to ignite a powder charge and send a cannonball flying. And all it takes is one small cannonball to take off a limb. Therefore, before taking any action, suffocate the cannon's air vent and use a damp mop—the one you've been swabbing the deck with will work just fine—to extinguish lingering sparks in the bottom of the barrel. Even if you're using a cold cannon, it's better to be safe than sorry. No amount of catgut and goodwill will get your skull mended or your arm reattached. Then again, if you're fighting a foe as fearsome as the Kraken, it might not matter anyway (see "How to Defeat a Sea Monster," page 146).

2. LOCK AND LOAD. Here comes the fun part. Once you're absolutely sure no live spark remains in your barrel, dump a charge of powder—

DAMP THE BARREL BEFORE ADDING POWDER

LOAD THE BALL, THEN STEP ASIDE

which usually comes in a handy premeasured bag—down the hatch. Use a ramrod to pack the charge before carefully adding your cannonball. Obviously, using the correct gauge is of utmost necessity: Too large a ball won't fit, of course, and if your ammunition is too small, it's likely to be thrown on an erratic trajectory and miss its target. Erratic may work for Jack Sparrow, but for cannonballs, it's not recommended. Once the ball is loaded, stick a fresh fuse into the air vent and get your torch at the ready. (You *do* have a torch at the ready, right? We thought so.)

3.   READY, AIM, FIRE. Despite the inviolable laws of physics and chemistry involved, the art of aiming a cannon is mostly intuitive. No measuring of wind, horizon, or pitch of your vessel can trump the gut judgment of a great artilleryman who's had lots of practice. Speed is of the essence when firing at the enemy, so don't overthink it; when your aim is true (as far as you can tell), light the fuse and move back. *Quickly.* A cannon's recoil is considerable, and you don't need to aggravate an already testy procedure by getting yourself run over by your own gun. It's really that simple, more or less, although there's no substitute for a decent amount of trial and error. Just make sure not to part company with more than a finger or two while mastering the subtleties of the art.

How to Board a Ship

Jack Sparrow is known far and wide for his magical exploits dealing with such fantastical surprises as the cursed sea captain Davy Jones, the Kraken, mermaids, and the Fountain of Youth. But a pirate's life isn't always so exotic. Some days you'll be seizing a plump, loot-laden galleon; other days you'll be preempting an invasion by some uniformed do-gooders. Either way, abruptly boarding other people's ships is a pirate's bread and butter. There's far more to the process than simply pulling up alongside and jumping over. Diligence, dexterity, and keen wits are needed to pull off a lucrative hijacking without getting jacked yourself.

1. KEEP YOUR EYES ON THE PRIZE. Every second counts, so the pirate who's first to spot another ship is the hero of the day. Many pirates—Captains Jack Sparrow and Hector Barbossa among them—see the size of one's spyglass as a measure of personal stature. That may seem silly, but it bears a certain underlying truth. Still, seeing as how the spyglass is a rather elementary device—after all, you only need to peer into the business end—the true skill comes in knowing *when* to use it. Have one on you at all times, both at land and on sea, and vigilantly scour the horizon for signs of predator or prey. If that means you're always whipping out your apparatus to show off your telescopic prowess, so be it.

ASSESS THE RISK YOUR PREY PRESENTS

2. GIVE CHASE. Once a potential prize is sighted, it's best not to rush it directly. Instead, pull back as far as possible and shadow the ship on a parallel course. By ghosting it in this way, you'll be able to observe pertinent details, such as: How armed does the ship appear to be? How laden with goods? Whose flag does it fly, and how many allies might be in the immediate area? After the risk is deemed worthy by consensus, pursuit can be begin in earnest. Now's not the time for sneaking about. Instead, swoop down on your prize like a gull on a guppy. Davy Jones was known to use this tactic, compounding his ship's terrible appearance with shock and awe.

3. STRIKE FEAR. As previously mentioned, musicmaking has more than just a recreational purpose onboard a pirate ship. Drum beating, horn blowing, singing, and dancing are all part of the fine traditions of vaporing and capering. Before beginning these tactics of terror, however, it's customary (and effective) to fire warning shots across the other ship's bow. Not only does this "greeting" let them know you mean business, it makes the crew skittish and edgy, which you can exploit to your advantage. Next comes the best part: hoisting the Jolly Roger. Any captain worth his salt will have already deduced that your ship belongs to buccaneers, but the Jolly Roger imparts a primal panic in the hearts of law-abiding folk. In fact, that grinning skull-and-crossbones (see "The Many Faces of the Jolly Roger," page 54) will do half the work for you. Jack Sparrow will be the first to tell you that letting a simple flag accomplish half your toil is in no way lazy or dishonorable, unless, that is, you want to call *all* acts of piracy lazy and dishonorable. Which, granted, is an argument that could be made.

4. MAKE THE LEAP. In most cases, a limited skirmish is the most you'll
    need to win surrender from the ship you intend to board. Surrender
    is indicated by a striking of the other vessel's flag; after that, it's time
    to grab some booty. Grappling hooks are the best way to secure your
    gunwale to theirs, after which it's a matter of using loose rigging to
    swing over the other ship. Dropping smoke bombs is the best way to
    sow pandemonium on deck, which only heightens the victims' ap-
    prehension and curbs their urge for violent retaliation. And speaking
    of violence: It's true that all manner of close-quarter weapons, not to
    mention the shrapnel-spraying shotgun known as the blunderbuss,
    have been used by pirates in extreme circumstance. But most pirates
    of even modest self-esteem view such brutality as wasteful and in poor
    taste. After all, victims who believe they have a chance of surviving
    their ordeal are much more likely to give up their treasure with min-
    imal resistance—which, really, is a win-win.

How to Operate Underwater

LIKE FINICKY CATS AND FINELY DRESSED LADIES, PIRATES HATE
TO GET WET. IN A PECULIAR WAY, JACK SPARROW MIGHT BE
CONSIDERED SOMETHING OF A CROSS BETWEEN A FINICKY CAT
AND A FINELY DRESSED LADY; ACCORDINGLY, HE GETS WET ONLY WHEN
ABSOLUTELY NECESSARY. BUT PIRATES ARE CREATURES OF THE SEA, AND
KNOWING HOW TO OPERATE UNDERWATER—WHETHER THERE BY
CHOICE OR SUBMERGED THROUGH NO FAULT OF ONE'S OWN—IS A
MUST. INDEED, PIRATES MUST BE ABLE TO MOVE THROUGH SEAWATER

ALMOST AS EASILY AS THEY DO THROUGH AIR. THEY CANNOT BREATHE WATER, OF COURSE, BUT POSSESSING AN APPARENTLY SUPERHUMAN KNACK FOR SUBMARINE ACTIVITY ONLY ADDS TO THEIR INTIMIDATING MYSTIQUE. IN THE LONG RUN, THAT MEANS LESS WORK AND MORE PLAY ON DRY LAND FOR YOU.

---

1. SWIMMERS NEVER QUIT. It is perhaps stating the obvious that non-swimmers shouldn't be allowed anywhere near a dock, let alone a pirate ship. You never know when that ship might be yanked out from under you or when you might need to beat a hasty retreat over the bulwark. As undignified as it may seem, taking swimming lessons at a local recreation center or YMCA is an ideal way to sharpen your strokes in a safe, controlled environment free of sharks, cannonballs, and sea monsters. Just remember that most livestock—parrots included—are frowned upon in public pools. Also, take particular advantage of the diving board. As a pirate, you will likely be forced to walk the plank at some point (at sword point, to be precise), and high diving is excellent training. In that case, the absence of a parrot will be a blessing. Cotton, the mute pirate on Jack Sparrow's crew, had a parrot that spoke for him and uttered such phrases as "walk the plank." That avian death sentence still rings in the ears of those who have survived that very stroll.

2. HOLD YOUR BREATH. Holding one's breath seems like it would be the most instinctive thing a person could do. And, yet, there is an art

PRACTICE MANEUVERS WHILE COLD AND WET

to it—one that's of particular use to the pirate. There exists no better method of surprise attack then surging from the watery depths, not to mention that untold treasures often lurk on the sandy seafloor (or even the shallower parts to which a human being might conceivably be able to dive). Ideally, you'll have plenty of time to prepare for an extended period spent below the surface; that way, you'll be able to inhale and exhale deeply and slowly for several minutes to stretch your lungs, oxygenate your blood, and calm your mind before the extreme stress your body is about to endure.

Of course, a pirate's life doesn't always afford one the luxury of time. In a pinch, hold and release as many huge lungfuls of air as you have time for. Before jumping into the drink, splash cold water on your face, which triggers a slow heart rate in mammals and ensures your body will make the most efficient use of its limited oxygen. Immediately before hitting the water, take one last breath and hold it. Don't completely fill your lungs, for that will hamper your swimming and make movement difficult. And, when rising from the deep, never pop to the surface too quickly; doing so can cause decompression sickness, also known as the bends. Nothing is less fetching in a pirate than joint pain, vertigo, vomiting, seizures, incontinence, and paralysis. If you're about to drown in an entirely other kind of liquid—such as the gooey spit and guts of the Kraken, as Jack Sparrow did—we can't really offer any advice.

3. ROCK THE BOAT. Submarines, scuba gear, even the ancient diving bell—none of these items are readily accessible to the pirate. But when it comes to breathing while moving around underwater, there is one device at the buccaneer's black fingertips: the boat. In a maneuver that

Captain Jack Sparrow made infamous (and, granted, few have at-tempted since), a small rowboat or dinghy can be carefully capsized so that air is trapped underneath. That way, a crew of two can walk the sandy bottom while hoisting the boat—with breathable air surround-ing their heads—above them. True, this crafty and unorthodox gam-bit requires nerves of iron and the ability to work well as a team. But it's entirely possible to secretly and safely reach a ship anchored off-shore by sneaking up on it in this manner. Just be cautious your oxy-gen doesn't run out; with two full-grown sets of lungs pumping away at a normal rate, the air trapped underneath an average dinghy will last only half an hour or so before lightheadedness, unconsciousness, and, ultimately, asphyxiation occur. You'll still be able to float to the surface; you just might not be alive to witness your own daring feat.

4. Join Davy Jones. "Do you fear death?" It's a question asked rhetor-ically and with no small amount of nefarious menace by the super-natural scourge known as Davy Jones. Many a seaman—pirate and sailor alike—has been netted and turned into a monster by the octopus-bearded captain of the spectral *Flying Dutchman*. Incredibly, others have entered his service willingly, gaining by association some small amount of his unholy power. For a crewmember aboard the *Dutch-man*, drowning is no real danger. After all, if you've struck a devilish deal with Jones—say, a captainship of your own one day in exchange for one hundred years of service to his evil endeavors—he'll not likely let you jump overboard and end it all before he's squeezed every last drop of life out of you. Furthermore, he'll have branded you with the magic mark known as the black spot, which means he can find you easily, even if, out

of sheer desperation, you do manage to part ways with his villainous ship. Drowning might seem like sweet release from the clutches of the *Dutchman's* deck, but you'll get no such comfort. Or, as Jones himself so horribly put it, "Life is cruel. Why should the afterlife be any different?"

THE PARTS OF A SHIP

1. BOWSPRIT	9. FORESTAY	17. MAINSAIL
2. BULWARKS	10. FORETOP	18. MIZZEN TOPMAST
3. CAPTAIN'S CABIN	11. HATCH	19. MIZZEN MAST
4. FORE TOPMAST	12. HULL	20. MIZZEN SAIL
5. FORECASTLE	13. KEEL	21. QUARTER DECK
6. FORECASTLE DECK	14. MAIN DECK	22. RUDDER
7. FOREMAST	15. MAIN TOPMAST	23. SHROUDS
8. FORESAIL	16. MAINMAST	24. YARD

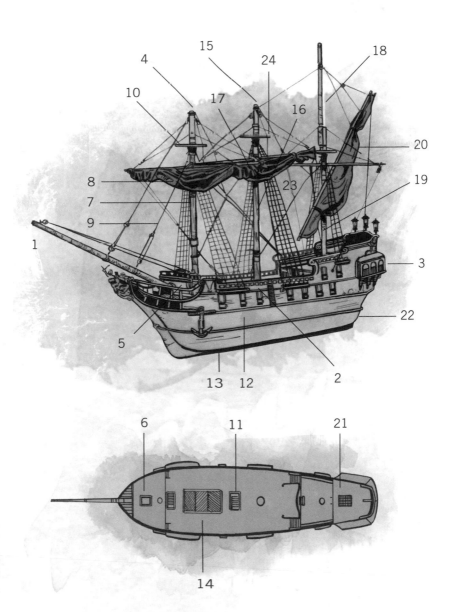

THE MANY FACES OF THE JOLLY ROGER

The grinning, luminous, skeletal visage of the Jolly Roger: In all the world, is there anything more terrifying? You'd better hope not. Pirates bank on the fear that famous flag strikes in the hearts of those sea voyagers they wish to liberate from material encumbrance. You're doing it all for their own good, even if they rarely see it that way. The Jolly Roger is a tasteful, tactful, and (may we add) rather fetching reminder that handing over one's valuables peaceably and without reserve is far preferable to the alternative. That alternative being, well—just look at the flag.

The skull and crossbones—allegedly first used and standardized by the infamous Edward England before being adapted with great aplomb by the Brethren of the Coast—is by far the most widespread and instantly recognizable rendition of the Jolly Roger. To be honest, though, the flag's appearance has just as often been mixed and muddled. The skull (or death's head, as it's better known to pirates) is indeed the most ubiquitous motif, although crossed pistols or sabers are occasionally substituted for the bones. Sparrow flies the skull and swords; Blackbeard was rumored to have a bleeding skull surrounded by flames on his Jolly Roger.

Another interesting—even poetic—image sometimes used was the hourglass. This symbol may not seem particularly threatening, but all wary ocean travelers knew full well what it meant: that time was of the essence, surrender was expected instantly, and the imminent pirate visit would only be worse if prolonged by those being visited.

Some pirates took the art of personalization to a whole new level. The aforementioned Bartholomew Roberts commissioned various designs depicting himself standing on two skulls and holding either an hourglass alongside a skeleton or a cutlass aloft. Did we mention pirates are vain?

Design wasn't the only consideration when designing one's Jolly Roger: The effect of the color was just as profound. A black flag, as petrifying as it is, is in fact the one the other ship would rather see, for it indicates quarter (life) will likely be granted to those about to be visited. Red flags mean the opposite: no quarter.

Just as its appearance has been mixed, so the Jolly Roger's deployment has been a scattershot practice over the decades. Hoisted

NOT ALL SKULLS ARE EQUAL

at the mizzen peak, the poop, or the topmasthead—or all three or some combination thereof—the flag is sometimes flown far in advance of an attack. Other times it's not flown until some other ruse has been tried, for example, flying the false colors of a friendly nation or company. Some especially puckish buccaneers have even been known to hoist it simply to clear a crowded harbor of ships in a hurry. Despite the Jolly Roger's inarguable beauty and power, such gratuitous advertising—particularly so near land—is hardly recommended. As Jack Sparrow himself will tell you, there's a time and a place to broadcast being a buccaneer. It's vital to keep in mind that merely having a Jolly Roger stowed in one's ship, or on one's person, is considered proof of villainy and punishable, in more severe municipalities, by imprisonment or worse. Possession, even for a pirate, is nine-tenths of the law.

SAILOR ESSENTIALS

1. BELAYING PIN
2. BLOCK & TACKLE
3. CANTEEN
4. CLEAT
5. COMPASS
6. HATCHET
7. KNIFE
8. NETTING
9. ROPE
10. SWAB
11. TAR

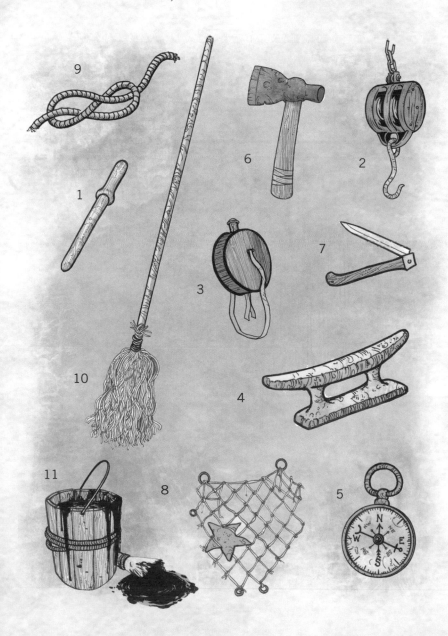

CHAPTER THREE

PEOPLE SKILLS

The practice of piracy can be a lonely sort of larceny—just ask Lord Byron's brooding, misanthropic Conrad from *The Corsair*, a literary hero we think shares a certain kindred spirit with Jack Sparrow (but that's just us). So, surrounding yourself with good comrades and competent crewmates is an urge as strong as plunder itself. Good news, buccaneers: Winning friends and influencing people is something at which pirates are particularly skilled. There's something about the irascible rogue that even the most prim and proper citizen finds irresistible.

In fact, even your fellow pirates—even your very enemies!—can fall prey to your piratical charisma, as long as you don't push it. Whether you're establishing your crew or dealing with those who would put you to the sword at the slightest provocation, people skills are among the most efficacious weapons in the pirate arsenal. Keep them sharp, and they will serve you well.

How to Recruit a Crew

THERE'S NO HR DEPARTMENT ON A PIRATE SHIP. ESPECIALLY ONBOARD THE BLACK PEARL. IN FACT, RELATIONS ABOARD SUCH VESSELS HAVE BEEN KNOWN TO GET DOWNRIGHT INHUMAN AT TIMES. HOWEVER, ONCE YOU DECIDE TO CAPTAIN YOUR OWN SHIP AND STRIKE OUT ON GRAND ESCAPADES ACROSS YOUR OWN PERSONAL CARIBBEAN, DRAFTING A CREW IS ESSENTIAL. PRESS-GANGING IS AN OPTION—IF YOU WANT YOUR THROAT SLIT AND YOUR CORPSE DUMPED IN THE WINDWARD PASSAGE IN THE MIDDLE OF THE NIGHT. NO, HIRING A FULL COMPLEMENT OF ABLE-BODIED AND, ABOVE ALL, WILLING HANDS IS THE BEST WAY TO OPTIMIZE YOUR ENTERPRISE. NO ONE'S SUGGESTING THAT YOU HAVE TO BE ENTIRELY HONEST ABOUT YOUR OPERATION WHILE RECRUITING YOUR CREW. WHAT KIND OF EXAMPLE WOULD YOU SET FOR YOUR NEW HIRES IF YOU DID?

1. SECONDS COME FIRST. Just as Jack Sparrow had the faithful (if somewhat sloshed) Joshamee Gibbs by his side, you, too, will need a right-hand man before you can seriously consider amassing a crew. Having a strong, stable, loyal second-in-command allows you to more quickly canvass the docks for available sailors and, perhaps more important, appear less desperate. Crewmates attract crewmates; knowing that you're not adrift on the tides of fate entirely alone makes your ship and your reputation more attractive. Also, the first mate—more often a quartermaster rather than someone with authoritarian experience—is likely to be more loved and trusted by the crew. In other words:

Your first mate works with you to play good cap'n/bad cap'n. (Fortunately, since quartermasters are naturally a stodgy, no-nonsense lot, your first mate has little chance of outshining you as a pirate, no matter how much the crew likes him.)

2. HEAD TO THE TAVERN. With your first mate in place, it's time to go fishing for crewmembers. And what better place to cast your line than into a rum barrel? Drunkenness in pirates may be frowned upon after anchors have been weighed, but, on dry land, the inebriated sailor is your salvation. Even the proudest seaman is sometimes brought low by circumstance—and, of course, by grog. Persons of low fortune and muddled judgment, not to mention disgraced ex–naval men, are ripe for conscription into the noble consortship of pirate life. All it takes is a few well-placed jars of rum or beer to sweeten the deal. (If you're afraid your lack of reputation will deter possible recruits, just dress up as someone else. Angelica disguised herself as Jack Sparrow in order to enlist a crew at the Captain's Daughter.)

Contracts must be drawn up in advance, of course—another duty ideally suited to a practical quartermaster/first mate—so that a quick signature can consummate the arrangement. Granted, upon awakening the next morning your new conscripts may not remember signing up for duty, but that point will be moot: They will already be in your hold, their contract stuffed in their pockets and a life of adventure ahead.

On a related note: Headhunting—that is, wooing away sailors already contracted to other captains—is perfectly acceptable, especially when your notions of ethics are as fluid as the high seas. Just be aware

AN OLD-SCHOOL MOTLEY CREW

that this particular term has a more literal meaning in the tropics, so avoid speaking it within earshot of your recruits. No one, not even the ugliest of pirates, is happy to lose his head.

3. GIVE THE SIGNAL. We've already discussed the telltale clues indicating that a person may be a pirate. We've also mentioned the pirate's love of song. So it stands to reason that buccaneers have a special tune they use to attract potential comrades. Though some dispute this story as apocryphal, the nursery rhyme "Sing a Song of Sixpence" has long been rumored to be a piratical call to action. No lesser a pirate than Blackbeard himself is said to have recruited crewman by singing or merely whispering the song, one whose meaning fellow Brethren would immediately understand. The coded clues are all there: Sixpence was Bluebeard's standard per diem for those serving on his ships; "a pocket full of rye" was their daily ration of whiskey; and "four and twenty blackbirds baked in a pie" signified the pirate's favored modus operandi of springing nasty surprises on loot-laden ships.

Many pirates, however, have a tin ear—no one ever called Jack Sparrow a songbird, regardless of his name—so singing may hardly be prudential. A more direct approach is the handshake. Pirates are far too sly to have a simple secret handshake, but if you're attempting to recruit someone and want to make sure he's of proper pirate stock, shake his hand, begin the phrase, "Take what you can," and see if he completes it with a hearty, "And give nothing back!" This motto will innocently inform a new recruit that you're a pirate; if he answers you in kind, you'll know that he's one too and ready to sign on. (If instead he appears puzzled, you just wasted a perfectly good mug of grog.)

4. LEVEL THE QUESTIONS. Finding crewmen is one thing. Finding good ones is another. Eagerness in a new recruit can be a blessing, but beware those who may be shipless for good reason. Naturally, you'll want a crewman who is experienced, physically sound, and, for lack of a better term, morally malleable. What you don't want is someone who appears too squeaky clean, regardless of credentials. Remember, you can teach a person to master the skills of piracy, but you cannot teach a person to be a rogue. That sort of worldview can rub off on others, it's true. But you don't always have the luxury of time and patience.

    Another reason to carefully screen applicants is to filter out potential mutineers. Does your interviewee jump at the chance to level obscenities and spew bile at his former captains? If so, what makes you think he won't do the same to you as soon as your back is turned? A little healthy venting among crew is fine and, at times, even beneficial. But there's a fine line between a sailor who utters grievances against his captain and one who instigates wholesale mutiny. Pirate ships are powder kegs, and that tension can sometimes be ignited by the spark of a single dissident. You don't want to have to start looking for a new crew all over again, do you?

5. BE AN EQUAL-OPPORTUNITY NE'ER-DO-WELL. Pirates are a superstitious lot (see "Top Five Pirate Superstitions," page 158), and one of their more unfortunate and unfounded beliefs is that bringing a woman onboard is bad luck. Angelica might have something to say about that, as would other notorious female pirates, like Mary Read, Anne Bonny, Grace O'Malley, Hannah Snell, and untold scores of others. Some, like Swann, started out in a corset and a frilly frock before

dressing openly as a pirate, whereas others disguised themselves as men from the start (see "How to Disguise Your Gender," page 77).

Being obligated to hide one's gender to serve as a pirate is, of course, ludicrous. In fact, it flies in the face of one of piracy's primary yet unspoken tenets: that social conventions and stereotypes are there to be shattered and that a pirate, of all people, should know better than to judge and look down on others. On a pragmatic level, a pirate captain does himself (or, of course, herself) a disservice by banning women. Some of the most daring and capable buccaneers have been female, and a policy of fairness and openness will augment your crew and attract the best and brightest blackguards to boot. That goes not just for women, but for pirates of all colors, shapes, sizes, backgrounds, and orientations. The best pirate ship is a melting pot. At all times, remember this: We outcasts, scoundrels, and buccaneer scum (to borrow the parlance of the lubber) have to stick together. Divided, we're nothing but chum for the sharks.

How to Impress the Locals

THROUGHOUT THE CARIBBEAN ISLANDS (AND BEYOND), YOUR SUC-
CESS AS A PIRATE OFTEN HINGES ON HOW WELL YOU CAN MOVE
AMONG THE NATIVE POPULACE. DOING SO IS HARDER THAN IT
SOUNDS: THESE ISLES HAVE BEEN CONQUERED, SETTLED, LIBERATED, RE-
COLONIZED, AND TAKEN BACK MORE TIMES THAN MOST PEOPLE CAN
COUNT. THE RESULT IS A RICH, RADIANT POLYGLOT OF CULTURES AND
PEOPLES. THE DRAWBACK? WHAT MAY PLACATE THE DENIZENS OF ONE
ISLAND MAY ENRAGE THOSE OF ANOTHER, AND OFTEN YOU'RE FORCED TO
LAND IN PLACES YOU'RE UNFAMILIAR WITH. HERE ARE A FEW TIPS TO
HELP INGRATIATE YOURSELF WITH THE LOCALS—AND THEN EXTRICATE
YOURSELF WHEN THE NEED ARISES.

1. ENTRANCES ARE EVERYTHING. You never get a second chance to
    make a first impression, and this is especially true for pirates. The way
    you enter a place establishes your image in the minds of the locals and
    can fix your reputation for years to come. Infamy cuts both ways, so
    be sure you're well aware of the type of image you wish to project
    before barging into a new town, village, settlement, ship, tavern, or ex-
    ploitative opportunity (see "How to Spin Your Own Myth," page 81).
    On the one hand, you might save a local beauty from drowning and
    thus find a grateful family—hopefully one well equipped with capi-
    tal—indebted to you. (Though that tactic didn't quite work for Jack
    Sparrow.) On the other hand, you might go marching into town with
    trumpets blaring, as did the great English privateer Sir Francis Drake

when he tried bluffing his way into the Spanish treasure houses of Nombre de Dios.

On that note: Creating utter confusion can be just as effective as establishing a specific identity. When in doubt, sow chaos and enter the scene in a billow of smoke, casting yourself as scourge, savior, or both at the same time. Ambiguity can be your friend—Sparrow is a prime and colorful example—and, in the long run, keeping people guessing about your true motives and methods often works better than simply pretending to be virtuous or evil. For aren't all humans, pirates included, a little bit of both? If the world is a stage—and for pirates, it most certainly is—then making a grand, loud swashbuckling entrance not only sensationalizes you in the eyes of the sympathetic, it throws potential enemies off balance long enough for you to turn and run.

2.   MAKE LIKE A GOD. Despite the gruesome reputation held by the island of Pelegosto (see "The Geography of the Caribbean," page 114), cannibalism is not widespread in the Caribbean; you're more likely to be killed and eaten by a shark than by a tribal native. With the teeming bounty of the Caribbean at your fingertips, why go through the trouble of eating people? Even for the natives of Pelegosto, a higher purpose than mere nourishment lies behind their occasional cooking of a fellow human. The tribe's legendary attempt to roast Jack Sparrow over an open fire was in fact a religious rite. After the *Black Pearl* ran aground there, Sparrow was clad and painted in the image of one of the locals' gods. Unfortunately, that meant eventually cooking and eating him as a way to pay tribute to the higher power.

Do not let this story dissuade you from impersonating a god—and reaping the rewards—if you think you can get away with it. Just do so with your eyes open, and always have an escape plan ready, should you smell a barbecue firing up.

3. AVOID ENTANGLEMENTS. Like a fish caught in a sailor's net or an albatross ensnared in the rigging, pirates, too, sometimes become tangled in affairs of the heart. These are not always romantic relationships; often they're simply soft-hearted reactions to petty injustices, innocents in trouble, and, yes, damsels (or lads) in distress. Despite their ferocious image, pirates are underdogs, too, and they occasionally become caught up in the righting of wrongs, mostly through no fault of their own. Some pirates even—horror of horrors!—fall in love. Although that *can* have a happy ending, it can just as often lead to tragedy of a superhuman sort. (But maybe Davy Jones should tell you about that; his tragic love affair with the sea goddess Calypso can reduce the most hardened pirate to a weeping babe.)

Indulging in the impulses of the heart isn't bad in and of itself—just beware making promises you cannot keep. It's easy to confess eternal devotion while in the throes of ecstatic passion. Yet the life of a pirate allows little room for such things, and you might wind up with a chest heavy with regret instead of treasure—or the slaps of a few irate, heartbroken strumpets across your cheek. Also, it is important never to mix business and pleasure. The anger of a jilted female can be quite potent indeed, but the anger of a jilted female pirate—such as Angelica—can be lethal.

STAY ABREAST OF LOCAL FASHIONS

How to Use Words to Misdirect and Confound

PIRATES—AT LEAST THOSE WORTH THEIR SALT—KNOW WELL THAT A SINGLE, WELL-PLACED WORD CAN WREAK MIGHTIER HAVOC THAN HURRICANE OR CANNONADE. THAT JACK SPARROW IS ABLE TO MANIPULATE OTHERWISE STRONG-WILLED FOLK IS TESTAMENT TO THIS FACT. VIOLENCE IS USELESS IN MANY SITUATIONS AND INAPPROPRIATE IN FAR MORE. WHY FIGHT WHEN YOU CAN FINAGLE, FLIMFLAM, FLIP-FLOP, FAST-TALK, FLEECE, FUDGE, AND DEFRAUD? ALL IT TAKES IS A GOOD THESAURUS—YES, THIS IS ONE INSTANCE WHERE LITERACY IS THE PIRATE'S FRIEND—AND LOTS OF PRACTICE, NOT TO MENTION A WILLINGNESS TO THRUST AND PARRY WITH WORDS RATHER THAN SWORDS. THOUGH IT TAKES DEDICATION AND DAGGER-SHARP WITS, A SLICK TONGUE CAN OPEN DOORS, UNLOCK SHACKLES, DIVERT SUSPICION, AND PUNCTURE THE SKIN IN A WAY NO WEAPON CAN. AND ALL WITHOUT SOILING YOUR FROCKCOAT OR BLOODYING YOUR KNUCKLES.

1. DON'T USE ONE WORD WHERE TWELVE WILL DO. Like a flag flown from the highest mast, your tongue must be unfurled and let loose upon the breeze. Speak, pirate, speak! Initiating a monologue in any situation allows you to take charge of the exchange, sets the tone for its duration, and keeps your adversary disoriented. If you're at a loss for what to say, ramble: Comment on the weather, the tide, politics real or

imaginary, and/or your adversary's sartorial elegance (even—no, *especially*—if there is a glaring lack of such). Keep the patter going. Speed and volume of verbiage, rather than quality, are your friends.

When you do find your tongue lagging, resort to the rhetorical (or even nonsensical) question, such as, "How does one remain well ventilated and dignified in this oppressive clime?" or "Are lavender petticoats after the Isobellan fashion still the rage in Hispaniola?" Naturally, you answer these questions yourself, preferably with a skyward squint and a distracted air, two of many such tactics practically trademarked by Jack Sparrow. Your exasperated adversary, his mind derailed by the heat, length, and loquacity of your wind, will have no room to reply, and that frustration will give you the chance to switch subjects and skate away from whatever offense you committed. Those keen on apprehending you may just as readily shoo you away before they realize what's happened. You'll have some breath-catching to do, but less so than if you'd had to fight and/or run away.

2. EVINCE OBFUSCATION. Big words: Most right-thinking folk hate and fear them. All the more reason why you should use them. Throughout history, many pirates have been educated persons with vast vocabularies at their verbal disposal, but it's the relatively unlettered Jack Sparrow who is most often associated with the fine art of logorrhea (or, to be clearer, a recrementitious lexicon). Hector Barbossa is also known for employing such a method.

Granted, big words can be just as daunting to the average pirate as they are to the average citizen. Just keep in mind that, even if you slip up, few people will know it. So don't worry about mispronouncing them, using them incorrectly, or inventing hitherto-unknown words entirely. That only adds another layer of obfuscation to the proceedings, which is exactly what you want. If you can practically hear the clockwork grinding away in your adversary's heads as they try to decipher your magniloquent diction, all's the better.

3.   HARNESS SARCASM. Sarcasm is the blunderbuss of rhetoric. Scattershot and imprecise, it often misses its target, hitting others you weren't aiming at or backfiring completely. That said, it's a powerful tool in your arsenal: Trenchant, acerbic speech is the pirate's preferred mode of conversance because of its tendency to amuse oneself and further confuse and imbalance whomever you're speaking to.

Of all the forms of sarcasm at one's razor-sharp tongue-tip, the backhanded compliment is the most sublime. Witness a favorite salutation of Jack Sparrow's: "And to what do I owe the pleasure of your carbuncle?" No one's carbuncle is in the least pleasurable, but when delivered with a florid bow and a devilish grin, a potentially hostile individual is immediately put on the befuddled defensive. As mentioned, however, sarcasm can get the better of you, so try to mean what you say at least some of the time. You never know when your life may depend on someone taking your words at face value—for example, "Help, I'm being attacked by a zombie."

How to Invoke the Right of Parlay

THE MOST EGREGIOUS MISAPPREHENSION ABOUT PIRATES IS THAT THEY HAVE NO MERCY. IN TRUTH, THE ACT OF CLEMENCY IS ENTIRELY WITHIN THE PIRATE'S REALM OF CONDUCT, ASSUMING THERE'S SOMETHING IN IT FOR THE PIRATE. THE RIGHT OF PARLAY, ONE OF THE ARTICLES OF THE PIRATE CODE, WAS DESIGNED TO KEEP PIRATES CAUGHT IN EXTENUATING CIRCUMSTANCES FROM COMPLETELY OBLITERATING ONE ANOTHER. LIKE ALL CIVILIZED SOCIETIES, THE ADMITTEDLY LOOSE FEDERATION KNOWN AS PIRATEDOM HOLDS COLLECTIVE SELF-PRESERVATION AT A PREMIUM, ALTHOUGH THAT DOES SOMETIMES CLASH WITH THE ENLIGHTENED SELF-INTEREST OF ITS CONSTITUENTS. WHEN THESE DUAL AIMS CLASH, PARLAY IS THE ANSWER. INVOKING IT IS NOT TO BE DONE LIGHTLY. HERE ARE GUIDELINES TO MEMORIZE LONG BEFORE THROWING YOURSELF INTO A SITUATION WHERE PARLEY MAY BE CALLED FOR.

1. CHECK THE FINE PRINT. The Pirate Code, as codified in written form in the *Pirata Codex*, is extremely specific about the Right of Parlay. Unfortunately, the codex is unavailable for perusal by the typical pirate. But it's safe to assume that, at some point in their careers, elders and those of higher rank within the Brethren have laid eyes on its padlocked, parchment pages. They will tell you that invoking this right forces antagonistic pirates to cease hostilities and take you to their captain to negotiate a more lasting truce or quid pro quo arrangement.

The thing to bear in mind is this: Parlay doesn't pertain to those who aren't members of the Brethren. Invoke parlay at a king's soldier or tavern keeper, and at best you'll get a blank stare, at worst a laugh. The inverse is also true; the right does not cover nonpirates, although sometimes it may suit your purposes to allow a civilian to *think* they're being protected by parlay. That said, the sanctity of parlay is so strong, most pirates are hesitant to break it even when a civilian *is* the one invoking it.

2. INVOKE AWAY. When you're certain the Right of Parlay is both applicable and advantageous to your situation, go for it. There's no need to get fancy: "I invoke the right of parlay"—leveled firmly, calmly, and with steely conviction—is the best way to pierce the fog of melee and freeze even the most bloodthirsty buccaneer in his tracks. Hopefully before he's run you through with his cutlass. The thick of battle, however, can often deafen those who have succumbed to a berserker rage; in such instances, the abbreviated exclamation "Parlay!" will suffice. If your life is in immediate danger, you needn't be calm. Go ahead and scream like a little girl.

3. DON'T OVERDO IT. Like the boy who cried wolf, those who invoke parlay too often risk lessening its impact. No matter how dire the situation, exhaust all other options—and then, think twice. Not only is it in poor form, you may wind up, ironically enough, damning yourself: Once you're known as a parlay-abuser, you'll be viewed by fellow Brethren as a bit of a lily-livered jellyfish. When that happens, no amount of parlay-begging for will save you. As the pirate Pintel of the

Black Pearl once swore, "If anyone so much as mentions the word 'parlay,' I'll have their guts for garters."

How to Disguise Your Gender

As previously discussed, a successful pirate captain will do well to realize that it's both equitable and expedient to hire associates of all backgrounds and appearances. (Even a ship as infamous as the Black Pearl is an equal-opportunity employer, and Captain Jack Sparrow is far from averse to the presence of women on his ship.) Still, it may be wholly to a female pirate's advantage to dress like a man. For instance, due to the demands of modesty or machismo, lucrative information may be revealed only in the presence of other men, or women may sometimes enjoy the economy and freedom of movement afforded by men's garb. And, as much as we hate to admit it, some pirate captains are still backward-thinking rapscallions prone to petty prejudices and the superstition against women on ships—in which case, what better ship to infiltrate, hijack, and strip for all it's worth?

---

1. CLOTHES MAKE THE MAN. Fair or not, clothing has long been used as a way not only to protect and express oneself but also to judge others. Women dressing as men should be careful to conceal their more feminine attributes within the shirts, boots, and breeches of the male dress

code, and to make sure those shirts, boots, and breeches project the desired image. Dressing as a magistrate or a dandy can open many doors for the disguised female pirate, but it can shut many others. Take careful stock of your situation, and dress accordingly.

Luckily, pirate history offers many cross-dressing role models. Already mentioned are Mary Read and Anne Bonny, though the most daring by far is Angelica. When Captain Jack Sparrow arrived in London, word had already spread like wildfire that he was there with a ship and planning to recruit a crew at the Captain's Daughter. Totally unaware of his own supposed intent, Jack ventured down to said pub, where he encountered his doppelganger: a dreadlocked, bearded, be-dongled lookalike, exhibiting a near-flawless execution of identity theft. It wasn't until real Jack began a duel with imposter Jack that real Jack discovered the truth: the swaggering copycat was actually Angelica in disguise. It might not be difficult for a woman to throw on a pair of breeches and smear a little soot on her face, but to impersonate such a unique character with such a signature style— now that takes talent.

2. WALK IT LIKE YOU TALK IT. Looking like a man is one thing; acting like a man is another. Pirates in particular are given to bouts of excessive manliness that almost make them a mockery of themselves. But when disguised as one, you want to appear as just another mate in the gang. Rather than trying to beat them at their own coarse, smelly, hairy game, it's better to master the practice of small mannerisms and tics. Pirates already have an undeniably rolling gait—Jack Sparrow more so than others; try to match it by mitigating the movement of

BOTH THESE PIRATES HAVE A SECRET

your hips and barreling around like a bit of a lout.

Even more important is your voice. There's no deader giveaway than lapsing into a womanly register. Always speak in a low and throaty tone, and refrain from talking altogether, if possible. If you're of the proper age, passing yourself off as a teenage boy can give you leave to explain accidental cracks in your speech. It also doesn't hurt to continually and crassly punctuate your discourse with belches, curses, and overall crudity. (If, that is, you don't do so already.)

3. CROSS-DRESSING SWINGS BOTH WAYS. Draping oneself in the sartorial trappings of the opposite sex offers the pirate many advantages, subterfuge being the most obvious. But there's another motive a pirate—especially a male pirate—might have for doing so: personal preference. Even the manliest of pirate captains enjoy a billowy silk shirt, an extravagant sash, and scads of glittery jewels, despite the challenge to keep such finery clean. It's been rumored that some pirates have gone so far as to experiment with dressing entirely in the lace and brocade of a woman. In fact, no less a legend than Bartholomew Roberts is said to have enjoyed the touch of a lady's gown. (Granted, it's more often rumored that Black Bart was a woman masquerading as a man.) And Jack Sparrow himself, while no cross-dresser, has always flirted with gender ambiguity. In any case, Sparrow's trusty mate Joshamee Gibbs was definitely known to shout orders to slacking crewman such as "Lift it like a lady's skirt!" Who's to say he wasn't talking about their *own* skirts?

FAKE IT TILL YOU MAKE IT

How to Spin Your Own Myth

CAPTAIN JACK SPARROW WILL BE THE FIRST TO TELL YOU: WHEN IT COMES TO PIRACY, APPEARANCES ARE FAR MORE IMPORTANT THAN ACCOMPLISHMENTS. HEARSAY AND APOCRYPHA CAN CARRY MORE WEIGHT THAN A GALLEON, AND BOASTS AND BLUFFS CAN PACK MORE FIREPOWER THAN A MAN-O'-WAR. A NIMBLE TONGUE IS A PIRATE'S GREATEST IMPLEMENT, BUT YOUR OWN TONGUE GOES ONLY SO FAR. THAT'S WHY YOU MUST CONJURE AND PROMULGATE A PERSONAL MYTH THAT'S SO BOLD, BOMBASTIC, FANCIFUL, AND OUTRAGEOUS THAT ALL WHO HEAR IT WILL EAGERLY SPREAD IT, EVEN AS FEW WOULD EVER BE TEMPTED TO ATTEMPT UNRAVELING FACT FROM FICTION. AND IF THEY DO TRY, YOU'LL HAVE

LONG SINCE ABSCONDED WITH YOUR BOOTY, SKIN, AND EVER-GROWING
MYTH INTACT.

1. EXAGGERATE, DON'T FABRICATE. Lying is a poor man's game (when, that is, it's not a dead man's game). Everyone lies, but most fibs are confined to the small, white, and/or banal variety. The epic, grandiose falsehood is the one most pirates are prone to indulge in. They're also the ones that will come back to haunt you, especially when you're unable to live up to them, a predicament that usually requires a still-larger lie and a larger lie after that, ad infinitum. Instead, employ the same light-fingered panache when handling the truth as you would when handling diamonds and doubloons.

When constructing one's own myth, start with a foundation of truth, real-life exploits that can be stretched and molded into something self-servingly fantastic yet still based in reality. For instance, Jack Sparrow—one of piracy's brassiest myth spinners and self-promoters—managed to convert a few lucky escapes from marooned islands and cannibalistic tribes into a vast and nebulous personal fable that preceded him everywhere he went. Awed deckhands would whisper reverentially about the time Sparrow rode the backs of two sea turtles to make his way off an island upon which he'd been cast ashore. And his sojourn in Davy Jones's Locker remains to this day one of his greatest myths—although in that strange case, Sparrow truly did perform a superhuman feat or two worth gossiping about.

2. BEND THE RIGHT EARS. Loose lips sink ships, but they can float a pirate's reputation, too. The problem is, there's something inherently untrustworthy and unsavory about spreading one's own myth. It's a good thing pirates are, by and large, untrustworthy and unsavory; a buccaneer who *doesn't* boast about his or her illicit handiwork is more suspect than one who does. But it's just that—idle boasting—unless you get others to do your talking for you. Spin your wild exaggerations and feed them to those who blather across fishing nets and back fences as a way of life. Even Jack Sparrow had Joshamee Gibbs to disseminate the outrageous, improbable details of his miraculous escapades, which Gibbs shared in hushed tones of conspiratorial reverence.

In other words: Don't be haughty. Some of your most effective mouthpieces may end up being fishwives, innkeepers, barmaids, and drunks, all of whom chitchat and spread scuttlebutt like old crones (especially when flattered or tipped outrageously). They're also relatively easy to impress and are avid, colorful embellishers, which means they can add spice to your myth that you might never have dreamt up yourself. As long as your ever-expanding legend issues forth from the mouths of others—even admitted gossipmongers—it seems less like self-promotion and more like legitimate ballyhoo.

3. NEITHER CONFIRM NOR DENY. When you send a myth about yourself into the world, it will one day, months or years later, come back to you. If you're ever confronted with a peculiarly preposterous account of your past exploits—perhaps by an admirer, a would-be ally, or even a potential enemy—play it straight. It's of vital importance not to show shock or alarm in the face of such balderdash, no matter

how unrecognizable the story may be; like the tossing of the waves, just roll with it. A cryptic smirk can do more to substantiate and propagate your myth than any claim of ownership. You don't have to buy your own hype—riding on the backs of sea turtles, as Jack Sparrow is said to have done, *is* a little much—but never let a flicker of doubt cross your face.

PIRATE HYGIENE (OR THE LACK THEREOF)

1. WORN-IN FINERY
2. NATURALLY BRAIDED HAIR
3. RECYCLED GARMENTS
4. BODILY FRAGRANCE
5. DISTINGUISHED TEETH
6. WELL-USED FINGERNAILS
7. RUM-PERFUMED BREATH

PIRATE HYGIENE (OR THE LACK THEREOF)

PIRATE INSULTS

Pirates are not known for niceties, as their propensity for rude, crude, demeaning insults vividly illustrates. Still, there's a certain camaraderie to the buccaneer's boisterous badmouthing. You won't be much of a pirate unless you can hold your own in a brotherly barrage of scorn, invective, and sheer blasphemy. Accordingly, many if not all of the following brickbats can be hurled as both compliment and insult, depending on the context and tone of voice. Be wary of how you level such words, and at whom; on a pirate ship in the thick of battle (or a session of rum-sneaking), fits of laughter can quickly turn to fisticuffs.

BILGE RAT: Vermin of all kinds are a vile reality on ships, especially on pirate vessels, where notions and applications of hygiene are one rung below literacy on the ladder of priorities (see "Pirate Hygiene [or the Lack Thereof]," page 84). Rats thrive in ships' filthy, fetid bilges, and thus they are the lowest form of life on board, except possibly the fleas on rats. Calling someone a bilge rat is serious indication that he may not be your favorite person.

BLACKGUARD: Irony is one of the pirate's better-developed senses, and that's certainly the case when it comes to the word *blackguard* (pronounced *blaggurd*), a derogatory term for a lawless scoundrel. Those who lob this epithet at a fellow pirate are guilty of being blackguards themselves; it's the proverbial case of the pot calling the kettle black. That's okay. Self-aware self-deprecation is a healthy trait for a buccaneer.

BOOTLICKER: There's no lower part of a pirate than his boot, and there's no lower man than the one who will lick it to gain favor. It's not a literal accusation, of course, but calling someone a bootlicker (also: heel-licker or toe-licker) is akin to saying that person is utterly bereft of dignity. Granted, all pirate ships have a chain of command, and someone must be at the bottom of that string; still, a pirate has his pride, and not even the greenest sailor should put up with such abuse from a so-called superior.

BUCKO: Although normally a friendly salutation traded by crewmates and even true friends, the term *bucko* can also be used as a grievous insult. When spoken with menace, through clenched teeth, and in a tense situation, the word takes on the opposite meaning. In fact, at its most venomous, it can be given and taken as a deadly threat, especially when spat out as a patronizing "me bucko."

CUR: Since we've already established that pets are, to some degree, part of everyday pirate life, calling someone a dog isn't exactly a dire insult. Calling someone a cur, on the other hand, is serious business. Curs are craven, inferior mongrels—most often mangy—and leveling such an accusation casts into doubt not only the person's qualities as a human being but those of his mother and father as well.

FECULENT MAGGOT: Use this one sparingly, because it's quite a potent curse. *Feculent* means "scummy" in the particular sense of "soiled by biological waste material," and a maggot is, well, a maggot.

KNAVE: In medieval times, the word *knave*—which is used to describe a servant boy, usually one serving royalty—once had a neutral connotation. But in the age of piracy, it has come to be defined as a dishonorable, shifty, even treacherous kind of person. A knave is also another name for the jack in a deck of playing cards, so calling someone a knave casts a slight pall of cardsharplike ill repute over them.

LUBBER: Most people on Earth are lubbers. Short for landlubber, the term has been used by seamen for centuries to poke fun at those lumbering men and women who are chained to the drudgery of dry soil. But when used against a fellow sailor or pirate, lubber is a slanderous claim of ineptitude and clumsiness in regard to one's own seaworthiness.

PRIVATEER: The use of the term *privateer*—especially as an insult—is specific, indeed. Privateers were the sea robbers given an official letter of marque by their home nation, which granted them the legal right to hunt, steal from, and destroy ships that belonged to a hostile nation's merchant navy. Many privateers were outlaws before and/or after being legitimized by a letter of marque, and it's this slippery, ambiguous line that has led many pirates to hold privateers in the highest contempt. In a sense, privateers were sellouts to pirate ideals, becoming the lapdogs of authority when it was most beneficial to them. Therefore, the word *privateer* is insulting only when uttered by a pirate on the other side of the law.

ROGUE: As with *blackguard,* the word *rogue* is levied by one pirate against another only with extreme irony. That said, the term has an almost affectionate overtone, particularly when exclaimed in a fit of mock outrage. After all, every pirate is a rogue: a vagrant, mischievous scamp who's looked down upon and seen as patently inferior by the world at large.

SALTY WENCH: Calling a woman a wench is a dangerous thing; the term is more or less synonymous with "lady of loose morals," and it's of the lowest character to drop the W-bomb with such an intent. Calling someone a salty wench—*salty* meaning "coarse and lewd"—is even worse. That said, pirates tend to use *salty wench* as a unisex, catchall insult that's equally (if not more) offensive to a man as it is to a woman.

SCALAWAG: Used to describe a villainous or mischievous person, the word *scalawag* (or *scallywag*) is practically interchangeable with *rogue.* It does roll off the tongue more playfully, so it makes a good insult for those moments when a little levity is warranted.

SCOURGE: A shortened form of "scourge of the seven seas," that is, a pirate known for inordinately savage and violent habits. The best pirates have evolved from the brutal practices of their predecessors, so calling someone a scourge is to dismiss him as a primitive throwback to a time when piracy simply wasn't fun-loving and swashbuckling.

SCULLION: No part of a ship is filthier, smellier, and sweatier than

KNAVES, CURS, OR MAGGOTS?

the kitchen, and in less civilized times a scullion was the subordinate worker in this miserable area. Most pirate ships have only a cook working in the galley, but the term *scullion* has remained an effectively acidic term when calling out someone who is filthy, smelly, and sweaty.

SCURVY DOG: Calling someone a cur is far more of an affront than calling them a scurvy dog, but there's still some life left in this old standby. The term is usually aimed at a group of carousers or layabouts; a pirate captain's cry of "Ye scurvy dogs!" can usually be heard like clockwork on the ship's deck. Yet a more serious basis underlies the seemingly mild insult: Caused by a lack of vitamin C, scurvy is the disease that strikes sailor and pirate alike, reducing both to weakened, toothless wretches.

SWAB: The verb "to swab" pertains to the scrubbing of the deck, a task assigned to pirate crewmembers with the least skill and seniority. A swab, therefore, is a term of disrespect that disparages a seaman's level of experience and, in a roundabout way, his intelligence. It also carries an intimation of cowardice, the idea being that those who swab the deck keep their heads down and out of trouble rather than joining in the fray—hence the appended insult "cowardly swab."

WRETCH: In many ways, calling someone a wretch is the most casually devastating insult you can fling. A wretch is a miserable human being, someone beneath contempt or, under normal circumstances, not even worth insulting. The fact that anyone—let alone a grand and prideful pirate—would deign to call someone a wretch means that person has truly and deeply earned the indignity.

CHAPTER FOUR

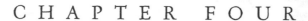

ACQUIRING BOOTY

Booty, loot, haul, hoard, trove: A treasure by any other name is just as sweet. Pirates amass treasure, it's as simple as that, and they revel in the skills and skullduggery required to liberate baubles and assets from those privileged individuals who surely are unable to properly appreciate such good fortune. But despite that legend and popular culture would have you believe most pirates are in it only for the booty, there's a deeper urge driving the swashbuckling freebooter. Aside from wealth, the great daring and danger required for its acquisition is an addiction that's hard to beat. Here are a few basic tips to ease your own procurement of the finer things in life. Just be sure to bear in mind that treasure is more a way of keeping score in the great game of pirating than anything else.

How to Loot

MORE THAN SAILING, SINGING, CURSING, OR CAROUSING, LOOTING IS A PIRATE'S LIFEBLOOD. THE BEST THING IS THAT YOU CAN SAIL, SING, CURSE, AND CAROUSE YOUR WAY INTO VAST MOUNDS AND GLITTERING CASCADES OF TREASURE—ASSUMING THAT YOU KEEP YOUR HEAD ABOUT YOU AND DON'T DEGENERATE INTO A COMMON BRUTE. REMEMBER, YOU'RE A SWASHBUCKLER NOT A RANSACKER. COMPORT YOURSELF WITH THE DIGNITY AND LIGHT TOUCH BEFITTING AN ELEGANT ROVER OF THE HIGH SEAS, FULL OF CHARM, WIT, AND GENEROSITY OF HEART. IN REALITY, YOU'RE HALFWAY TO BEING AKIN TO THAT MOST VALIANT OF OUTLAWS, ROBIN HOOD; YOU'VE SIMPLY DECIDED, IN THE INTEREST OF EXPEDIENCY, TO CUT OUT THE "GIVE TO THE POOR" PART.

---

1. REACH AN ACCORD. Surrender is such an ugly word. And yet, it's more or less what you're asking the captain of a prize ship (or the holder of a landlocked treasure) to do—not to surrender themselves but rather their most valuable assets. The secret is to avoid all threats: material, physical, psychological. Granted, the study of psychology did not exist by that name during the heyday of Captain Jack Sparrow. Yet he, like all pirates, understood it, and that understanding will suit you just as well. A threat evokes a reaction, often violent in passion or action, and violence must be avoided at all costs, as should bickering. You want to present your terms firmly and clearly, yet with a cavalier charm that tells your victim: "Let's all be reasonable people here, eh?"

It's also worth remembering that merchant captains rarely own all—or even part—of their cargo, which means that it's their reputation that is mostly at risk.

It's risky if the crew and/or passengers of a boarded ship witness their heroic leader buckling under the pressure of piratical demands; they might exhort him to stand up for their rights, or even try to take matters into their own hands. Take the captain aside, wink at him as if he were a coconspirator, wave away any noble and chivalrous protestations, and ask him point-blank, "Do we have an accord?" When presented as an arrangement between gentlemen rather than wholesale sea robbery at sword point, the whole operation will go much more smoothly. The same goes for operating on land. Of course, you do want to have a sword or two (or seventeen) lying around somewhere—perhaps nestled in the sashes and scabbards of the dozens of rogues, knaves, blackguards, and scourges standing behind you.

2. SLIP THEM THE SPOT. Okay, say you've tried the whole "reach an accord" thing, and it just isn't working. In fact, all you've managed to do is rile and mortify the ship's indignant captain, passenger, or property owner. Threats may seem like the quickest and most direct route, but even if you absolutely must resort to that rare extreme, don't rattle your saber or snarl like a beast. As a pirate, you are above such primitivism. Besides, you have the spot.

The black spot consists of any dark smudge—tobacco juice is fine, squid ink works well, but tar is probably the easiest and most abundant on any ship—smeared onto a piece of paper or parchment. Though not as ominous as the capitalized Black Spot given to Jack Sparrow by

Davy Jones (see "The Black Spot," page 163), this lone, deathly symbol tells your victim, "A dark, empty void is your fate if you don't get cozy with the idea of surrendering." Some of the more bookish and high-blown Brethren will pen an entire carefully worded threat below the smudge, letting your victim know exactly what kind of surrender is expected. Who has the time? Like a bank robber passing a note to a teller, you're in a bit of a hurry. Let the smudge speak for itself; in fact, it's far more effective when not diluted by scribbled text. Use the black spot as a kind of pocketsize pirate flag, ready to be unfurled at a moment's notice to strike fear and obedience in the hearts of your newfound, richly appointed friends.

3. BOOTY IS IN THE EYE OF THE BEHOLDER. Once you've acquired—through peaceful negotiations, accords, handshakes, and/or black spots—a certain docility in those you're looting, it's time to find the booty. It's a bit of a misapprehension that pirates are only on the lookout for gold. Many—such as Jack Sparrow, whose gold is mostly in his dental work—are just as partial to silver, more for aesthetic reasons than anything else. True, doubloons and pieces of eight will never be turned down by a buccaneer, but treasure isn't always so pretty, shiny, or glamorous. Many ships trading throughout the Caribbean are indeed carrying precious metals from the Spanish Main—metals that, it must be remembered, didn't belong to Spain in the first place—but more mundane items are also worth absconding with. Silk, wool, linen, tea, sugar loaves, molasses, and rum are all common goods that a pirate can either use himself or use to barter for something better.

Gold, however, is indeed the *first* thing you should look for. Definitely gold. Head to the hold first, since the weight of treasure chests is usually used as ballast to help keep ships steady and secure in tumultuous seas. If you hit the jackpot, dance a jig. Don't be shy. You've earned it . . . more or less.

4. IT TAKES A VILLAGE TO PILLAGE. Despite the ostensible paradox, there is a morality to looting. You and your crew are in this together—all for one and one for all, as a trio of vaguely pirate-looking fellows has been known to say. It's all well and good to present a chaotic, animalistic front to outsiders; the crew of the *Black Pearl* built their entire reputation on such a ghastly facade. But behind that image you must maintain order and mutual respect, if for no other reason than to keep your crew from pilfering from one another, plotting mutiny, or just plain jumping ship. There's just one way to do this: Share and share alike.

As we've mentioned before, any pirate captain worth his parrot divides booty equally among his crew. That requires a certain amount of trust and camaraderie, and the only way to foster this feeling is to lead by example. Sure, it's tempting to pocket an ingot of silver from the mines of La Taja de Plata or a pouch of gemstones from a Toltec tomb. But it's better to be a team player: After stripping a ship of its valuables, bring them—every last gleaming speck—to the communal treasure pile to be divided equally among the crew. A pirate ship, after all, is too close of quarters in which to double-cross one's brothers. To the victors go the spoils, but to the greedy goes the plank.

How to Smuggle

LOOTING MAY BE THE PRIMARY SOURCE OF A PIRATE'S INCOME, BUT YOU CAN'T EXACTLY TAKE YOUR STASH TO THE BANK. BEFORE YOU CAN SAFELY STOW IT (SEE "HOW TO BURY A CHEST," PAGE 101), YOU NEED TO SNEAK IT PAST THE PESKY, BLOODSUCKING OFFICIALS THAT INFEST ALL HARBORS OF REPUTE. THE PROVINCIAL AND IMPERIAL GOVERNMENTS OF ISLANDS ACROSS THE CARIBBEAN LOVE TO CHARGE AN ARM AND A PEG LEG FOR ANY INCONSEQUENTIAL SERVICE OR TAX THEY CAN DREAM UP; BERTHING FEES, PORT TARIFFS, AND WHARF HANDLING FOR THE MOORING OF WATERCRAFT ARE JUST A FEW OF THEIR GRATUITOUS LEVIES. AND THEN THERE'S THE SMALL, NIGGLING FACT THAT, TECHNICALLY SPEAKING, YOU'RE CARRYING PLUNDERED GOODS. AVOIDING SCRUTINY, FEES, AND TEDIOUS RECORDKEEPING IS THE AIM OF EVERY SMUGGLER. EVEN THE MOST RUDIMENTARY SMUGGLING SKILLS CAN SAVE AN HONEST, HARDWORKING PIRATE FROM BUSYBODIES, TAX COLLECTORS, AND WHOLLY UNWARRANTED SEARCHES AND SEIZURES. AFTER ALL, WHEN YOU DRESS AND CARRY ON AS FLAMBOYANTLY AS JACK SPARROW, YOU'RE A SHINY TARGET FOR EVERY SOBER, FUSSY, FRUSTRATED OFFICIAL THROUGHOUT THE CARIBBEAN.

---

1. STASH AND STOW. No true man or woman of the sea trucks a stowaway, unless said stowaway happens to be a chest full of riches. If your vessel is boarded by authorities or forced to moor in a so-called civilized harbor, the first thing they'll be looking for is booty. So don't leave it lying around. Your treasure should already be stashed as ballast

in the hold, but don't think that's good enough. Tax collectors can ferret out gold like the Kraken can spy the Black Spot, and it's up to you to construct false panels in the hull in which to conceal your hard-gained loot. The commode is another handy (if unpleasant) place in which to hide valuables, as is the bottom of any wormy barrel of hardtack. If worse comes to worst—and if you happen to have small yet highly valuable pieces of booty, like, say, diamonds—there's always the option of swallowing them. We don't recommend it, however; if you think the cook's turtle stew gave you indigestion, just wait until you try (and fail) to digest a gullet full of gems. Then wait until the morning after. Most treasure simply isn't worth that kind of hardship.

2. KNOW YOUR COASTS. Geography may seem a dry and dusty subject more fitting for pupils than for pirates, but a little topographical knowledge can go a long way (see "The Geography of the Caribbean," page 114). Luckily, it's easy to bolster one's education with a few maps—which can be purchased discreetly at any port or liberated from another ship—plus a modest investment of time and attention. An island's perimeter is likely to be pockmarked with shallows, banks, inlets, and coves, many of which are unpopulated and patrolled by only occasional agents of authority, such as Jack Sparrow's sometime nemesis James Norrington. Aside from established "pirates' coves"—traditionally, hidden places where the Brethren can meet, lay low, hunt, gather, and plot their next escapade—an intimate knowledge of the more out-of-the-way spots in the Caribbean's hundreds of isles ensures a never-ending supply of secluded places to bring ashore the fruit of one's plunder. It also helps to hug the coast when pursued by pesky

soldiers or merchant companies out for revenge. The cozier you are with that coastline, the better.

3. GREASE SOME PALMS. Palm trees sway in abundance in the warm, sweet Caribbean breezes, but those are not the kinds of palms a pirate cares about. Greasing palms—that is, establishing a quid pro quo with customs and tax officers, rather than evading them—is definitely a desperate, last-ditch measure. But when you're running rum or trying to snake contraband into a mainland or island, sometimes it's worth having an accomplice on the inside. *Bribe* is such an ugly word; think of it instead as forming a new business partnership—or even making new friends. Just be cautious when approaching potential partners with such overtures; look for the shiftiest, shabbiest clerk or inspector, and use the same kind of sixth sense you employ while sniffing out a fellow pirate. You never know: You may end up opening the poor fellow's eyes to the world's grandeur and adventure and turn him into a real pirate.

4. SMUGGLE SOLO. Given the pirate's nefarious—and, of course, wholly exaggerated—reputation as an utter, unprincipled scoundrel, there are people in the world set on exploiting your God-given buccaneer talents. It's a sad fact that often pirates are, paradoxically, victims of greedy scams and schemes by those scoundrels with none of a pirate's undervalued (though admittedly scant) scruples and morals. If someone approaches you with an offer that's too good to be true—namely, smuggling something across the Caribbean, a so-called easy job for a hefty fee—refuse. Far too many pirates have been apprehended on the ocean with contra-

band that's far too risky even for a hardened freebooter. In fact, steer clear of working with any nonpirates in any capacity, inasmuch as you're able; that goes double for the scurvy dogs of the East India Trading Company. As Jack Sparrow and many other pirates have learned on many an occasion, the wiliest and wickedest sea serpents often wear official uniforms of one kind or another, and collaborating with them in any way is not only a compromise to a pirate's principles but also in very poor taste. Piracy may love company, but you're not that desperate.

How to Bury a Chest

DESPITE THE OVERWHELMING AMOUNT OF FOLKLORE TESTIFYING TO THE PRACTICE, SOME PIRATOLOGISTS QUESTION WHETHER PIRATES LIKE JACK SPARROW, HECTOR BARBOSSA, AND THEIR CONTEMPORARIES REALLY EVER BURIED THEIR TREASURE. TO THOSE PEOPLE WE SAY: KEEP ON THINKING THAT. THE MORE DOUBTING THOMASES WHO DON'T BELIEVE IN BURIED BOOTY, THE BETTER THE CHANCES THAT WE WILL BE THE ONES TO DIG IT UP.

Besides the sheer romanticism of tucking one's gains (ill-gotten or otherwise) in a hole in the ground, the technique is a pragmatic one, enabling a pirate to escape a sticky situation unencumbered by huge amounts of contraband. But, as these tips will tell you, there's more to it than just sticking stuff in a box and sprinkling some dirt on top.

1. PICK THE BEST CHEST. The sea chest is a carefully considered storage solution; when plundering a ship, you can't just fill up your pockets with loot. One, pockets aren't big enough, even if you dress as extravagantly as Jack Sparrow; and two, a seafarer weighed down with gold is considerably more likely to drown in an unexpected fall (or toss) overboard. So pirates take the sturdiest nautical trunks—the kind found in the cabins of most oceangoing vessels—and remove the passengers' clothes and personal items to make room for jewelry and coin. Chests come in a wide variety of quality and construction. Try to find one made from good, soft wood, like pine (oak will be too heavy), and bound in rust-resistant brass, the shipbuilder's alloy of choice. Don't bother hunting down the owner to extort the key, since anyone who can find your buried treasure will be able to break a lock.

2. LOCATION, LOCATION, LOCATION. Finding the ideal hiding spot is essential. You want a low-traffic area, but one that's not so remote as to be inaccessible. For instance, Davy Jones buried his Dead Man's Chest on the deserted island of Isla Cruces, which travelers avoided because of a plague that had struck years before; *he* knew where the treasure was, and he knew it wouldn't be bothered. On the other hand, sometimes hiding an object in (almost) plain sight is better than being conspicuously inconspicuous—not to mention that you have to make your way back there one day to unearth it. Beaches are traditional burial sites, but a few hundred yards inland is better, where foliage and a lack of bathers will make for more permanent landmarks and help hide your chest of booty from prying eyes (and feet). Under no circumstances should you bury treasure on private property: that's trespassing, which can lead to all kinds of

sticky situations with the landowner—not the least of which is *them* now having a legal claim to *your* gold!

3. BRING THE RIGHT TOOLS. Shovels come in a wide range of shapes and sizes, and not all are suited to your particular task. Look for a sharp, medium-width blade—no more than 13 inches wide—that can slice tree roots and cut through varying densities of soil without sacrificing volume. The sheer amount of earth you'll need to move is prodigious, so a bucket will also come in handy. Don't underestimate hand tools, like trowels and three-pronged digging forks; they will help you break through tough soil and tenacious grass. Your most important tool, however, is a humble pair of gloves. Once broken in, good leather gloves will help prevent the blisters that are nigh unavoidable when digging. Despite popular myth, talcum powder sprinkled inside gloves won't help; though it reduces friction for a few minutes, it will soon add to the chafing. Oh, and one more thing: A sword—even one crafted by Will Turner, an expert blacksmith before becoming a pirate—makes a lousy shovel. Sorry.

4. DIG DEEP. (BUT NOT TOO DEEP.) The last thing you want is for some wandering lout to stumble across a corner of your chest after a rainstorm or windy day. Granted, there's little you can do to control natural erosion—other than digging a deep, deep hole. Since stealth and speed are paramount, you want to be as efficient as possible, but be wary of obstacles (like rocks). Also, do your research: Find out the depth of the local water table (the level below which groundwater saturates the earth). If the science becomes a stumbling block, consult

the obeah insights of Tia Dalma (see "Calypso," page 164). The last thing you want to do is stuff your treasure chest into a flooded hole; the brass will remain intact (albeit soon tarnished), but the wood will quickly rot, making for a messy disaster when you dig your treasure back up again.

5. **X SHOULD NOT MARK THE SPOT.** As strong as the temptation is, don't leave any kind of mark onsite to remind you where your treasure is buried. Replace any turf you removed before digging the hole and brush away boot prints left behind. Furthermore, don't make a symbol in stones or carve your initials on a nearby tree. There are other scoundrels—fellow pirates, adventurers, and authorities—who will come looking for your booty, and they know how to recognize such telltale signs. What you need instead is a map (see "How to Make a Treasure Map," page 109). Don't wait too long after burying your treasure before drawing your map; many a reckless and hasty pirate has dug his hole, dumped his booty, covered it up, and celebrated his triumph long into the night. The next day, he can't even remember where he buried it.

How to Gamble

ONE OF THE ARTICLES OF THE PIRATE CODE FOLLOWED BY JACK SPARROW AND HIS CREW CLEARLY STATES THAT IT'S FORBIDDEN FOR THE BRETHREN TO GAME AT CARDS OR DICE FOR MONEY. TO A PIRATE, THOUGH, RULES ARE SLIPPERY THINGS—AND SO IS THE DEFINITION OF "MONEY." IF YOU'RE MOST RECENT HAUL HAPPENS TO HAVE NET-

GO INLAND TO FIND A LANDMARK

THE RIGHT TOOLS FOR THE RIGHT DEPTH

TED A FEW BARRELS OF MOLASSES AND A DOZEN BOLTS OF THE FINEST ASIAN SILK, THAT'S NOT EXACTLY CASH ON THE BARRELHEAD, IS IT? THE FACT IS, GAMING AND GAMBLING ARE MARITIME PASTIMES AS OLD AS SAILING ITSELF, AND THOUGH IT DOESN'T HURT FOR A PIRATE CAPTAIN TO TRY TO QUASH SUCH ACTIVITY AMONG HIS CREW, THE BEST HE CAN DO IS CURB IT. SURE, DEFINING "MONEY" AS COIN ONLY IS PLAYING SEMANTICS—BUT THAT'S AN-OTHER GAME ENTIRELY. ANYWAY, A HUMBLE PIRATE SUCH AS YOURSELF DOESN'T KNOW SEMANTICS FROM SEAWATER, SO WHERE'S THE HARM? THE BOTTOM LINE IS, IT'S BETTER TO SETTLE BOREDOM AND PETTY SCORES ON A PIRATE SHIP BY GAMBLING RATHER THAN GUNPLAY. AND FEW PIRATE CAP-TAINS WILL SURVIVE LONG ON THE JOB WITHOUT ALLOWING THE CREW A LITTLE CODE BENDING—AND YOU CAN BET ON THAT.

---

1.   IT'S IN THE CARDS. Dignified seamen of the Royal Navy may pursue such gentlemanly diversions as chess and backgammon, but a pirate prefers playing cards. Cards are more versatile, more portable, and far less expensive—unless you're on the losing end of a hand of poker, the most ubiquitous and adaptable card game a pirate can play. Varia-tions on poker abound, but pirates of the most daring stripe favor Blind Man's Bluff, in which you can see every player's cards but your own. Even more adventuresome is Basset, usually considered a game for the wealthy because of its extreme monetary risk but played with a perverse sort of recklessness by the salty pirate.

Of the other popular wagering games popular during piracy's golden age, Lansquenet is a favorite, as is Piquet; the latter fares poorly in a crowded mess full of rowdy pirates hungry for sport, since it's designed for only two players. Whist is another agreeable choice, assuming the house rules can be clearly defined and agreed upon. The last thing you need is a civil war onboard when all you wanted to do was pass a little time (and perhaps lighten the purses of your brothers).

2. LIVE AND LET DICE. Pirates don't partake of backgammon, but one component of the game is worth purloining: the dice. Handheld and easily concealable, dice are the perfect gaming tools—and the natural rolling of a ship's deck adds a new dimension to the game. Craps is the fallback; simple to play, quickly paced, and perfect for a group of any size, it offers the advantage of being easily concealed when there's risk of being discovered by a particularly stiff-necked captain. As its name implies, the game known as Ship, Captain, and Crew has become a pirate-ship staple, as has Crown and Anchor, played with a unique set of symbolized dice that trickled down to the Brethren from sailors in the Royal Navy and British merchant fleets.

Yet most associated with pirates is Liar's Dice. This game goes hand in hand with drinking, and betting usually takes the form of monetary wager and alcoholic dare. It is a harrowing and high-stakes contest, as Jack Sparrow's comrade Will Turner can attest. Turner infamously challenged Davy Jones to this game, and in so doing managed to find the location of the Dead Man's Chest. Nevertheless, we do not recommend challenging Davy Jones. To anything. For any reason. Ever. The bones that get rolled may be your own.

3. DON'T TAKE CREDIT. Pirates pride themselves on standing on their own two legs—be they flesh and blood or merely wood—and yet many a buccaneer has succumbed to gambling fever. When plunder is dry and funds are scarce, pirates have been known to gamble on credit, using lead markers in place of coin. (Jack Sparrow also bets with his own soul in the pot, but that's another folly entirely.) When the time comes to pay the piper, some otherwise sober and sensible pirates have wound up losing the shirts off their backs—literally. In fact, some pirate ships have gone bankrupt this way. Remember: Pirates are in the pirate business to amass treasure, not to wager it away. The last thing you want to do is pour all your loot into a bottomless pit of debt. Chains of any kind are for lubbers.

4. TO CHEAT OR NOT TO CHEAT. Wickedness leads to wickedness, or so the pious would have you believe. That said, a slippery slope accompanies cheating at cards or dice. Jack Sparrow can play loose and devious with the rules when it comes to the grand game of life, but even he thinks twice about stacking decks or loading dice. Cardsharps and dice loaders are two of the most loathed denizens of the pirate world, and such hornswogglers, when discovered (and they always are), are often summarily keelhauled. Granted, card games invite some small amount of cheating; unless you're using newfangled reversible court cards (face cards that appear the same regardless of which way they're turned), it's expected that the approximate strength of your hand can be glimpsed by your opponents as you orient your cards. But even that is a fine distinction, not something upon which you would want to stake your reputation as a pirate—or as a breathing human being.

How to Make a Treasure Map

EXACTLY HOW DO YOU FIND THAT TREASURE AGAIN ONCE YOU'VE BURIED IT? SOME OF THE RICHES AND CURIOS YOU LIBERATE—SAY, A GOLD AZTEC IDOL OR AN EMERALD-CRUSTED NATIVE HEADDRESS—ARE LIKELY TO BE INSTANTLY RECOGNIZABLE ANYWHERE IN THE CARIBBEAN, WHICH MEANS YEARS MAY PASS BEFORE YOU CAN SAFELY DIG THEM UP AND SHOP THEM AROUND. THE ANSWER, THEN, IS A MAP. BUT DON'T THINK THAT SCRIBBLING A SKETCHY COASTLINE AND A BIG X ON THE BACK OF A NAPKIN IS GOING TO AVAIL YOU. HERE ARE A FEW TIPS TO HELP MAKE THE MAPPING MERRIER.

---

1. GET HELP (THEN GET RID OF IT). Cartography—the art of drawing maps—is no job for a layperson. It's a careful, precise science that takes years of training, libraries full of knowledge, and oceans of patience. As a pirate, you have none of these things—and if you're anything like Jack Sparrow, your fingers aren't steady enough for such a delicate craft. It's nothing but folly to believe you can successfully map the back of your hand, let alone half the Caribbean. So seek help. A cartographer isn't someone who sets up shop in a convenient location between every blacksmith and fishmonger, but a few well-placed pieces of eight in the hands of local merchants or missionaries should get you started in the right direction.

   Once you've secured their services and dispensed with the mapmaking, your next step is to ensure they don't try to dig up the treasure themselves. Seeing as how most cartographers are pusillanimous, deskbound jellyfish—not to mention chronically undercompensated—it should be no problem to bribe or blackmail them into keeping quiet. And keeping their shovels to themselves. After all, if your treasure comes up missing, they'll be the first one you'll come looking for.

2. KEEP IT CLOSE. The only problem with having a treasure map is the possibility of losing it. If you need to draw a map just to find the original map, you're doing something wrong. There are a thousand spots in which a map can be hidden, so pick the one that works best for you: a hollowed-out sword hilt, beneath the false bottom of a chest, and even inside the lining of your tricorne. Just be wary of duplicates. First, by the act of transcription you risk jumbling and misinterpreting the delicate details of the map. Second, the more copies of your map there are floating around, the better the chances it will be discovered (and your treasure will be pilfered). And in the name of all decent and worthy pirates, don't check your map every five minutes. If you covet your treasure that much, just dig it up already—or keep it in a simple box, like Davy Jones does for his heart.

3. GET IT IN INK. It's all very romantic to have a pirate map drawn on a piece of yellowed, weathered parchment—one that looks like it's been chewed up and spit out by the Kraken. But who's to say such a brittle document won't completely dry up and crumble to dust by the time you can use it? There is an alternative, at least for those with a high tolerance for pain: a tattoo. Getting your map inked onto your body is an ideal way to avoid the natural disintegration of paper (not to mention your fellow pirates' inclination to borrow the map for a few days).

LOCATE A CAREFUL TATTOOIST

FLIP IT FOR MIRROR READING

Just remember: Even if you're a vain type like Jack Sparrow who loves to show off your new ink, avoid getting your treasure map tattooed on a conspicuous stretch of skin. Between the shoulder blades is probably best, so it can be easily viewed with a mirror (assuming the tattoo is done in reverse; otherwise you'll be halfway to Iceland before you realize you're sailing in the wrong direction). Your forehead may seem like a fine canvas, but it's not going to keep the location of your treasure a secret for long.

THE KEY TO A PIRATE'S MAP

1. BEACH
2. BODY OF WATER
3. BRIDGE
4. CLEARING
5. CLIFF
6. DOCK
7. GRASS
8. JUNGLE
9. MOUNTAIN
10. QUICKSAND
11. RIVER
12. ROAD
13. SHIP ROUTE
14. TOWN
15. TRAIL
16. TREASURE
17. UNFRIENDLY/OVERLY FRIENDLY NATIVES
18. VILLAGE
19. WATERFALL

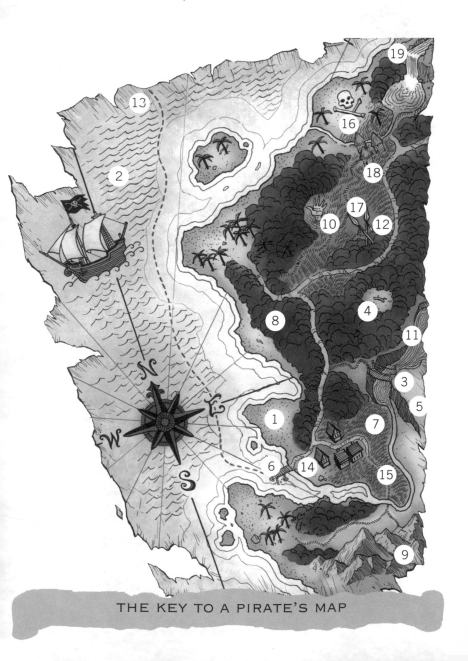

THE KEY TO A PIRATE'S MAP

THE GEOGRAPHY OF THE CARIBBEAN

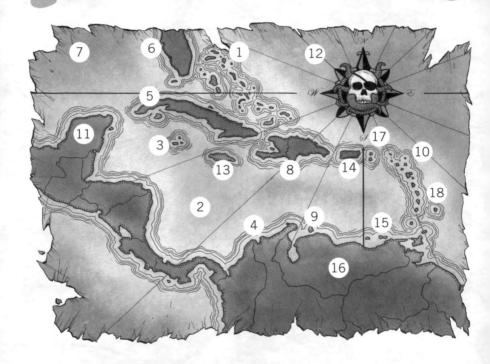

1. Bahamas	8. Hispaniola	14. Puerto Rico
2. Caribbean Sea	9. Leeward Antilles	15. Tortuga
3. Cayman Islands	10. Leeward Islands	16. Venezuela
4. Colombia	11. Mexico	17. Virgin Islands
5. Cuba	12. North Atlantic	18. Windward
6. Florida	13. Port Royal,	Islands
7. Gulf of Mexico	Jamaica	

PIRATE CURRENCY

Pirates are neither bankers nor accountants. And yet, you might need to think like one or the other to be able to decipher the complex, ever-changing, and often arbitrary system of monetary exchange used throughout the Caribbean. The confusion arises from the region's de centralized currency. It can hurt a poor pirate's head to juggle numbers in such a way, but one of the two major denominations of coin—the *doubloon*—is a slang word whose interpretation is open from island to island and from pirate to pirate. The term is rooted in the Spanish word for "double," and since each successive denomination of Spanish coins rises in value by a factor of two, a doubloon could (and often does) mean just about anything, although the commonly agreed-upon value is now considered to be 16 pieces of eight (see below). Nonetheless, doubloon does have a nice ring to it—both the word and the coin.

The other major denomination used by pirates is the *piece of eight*. Thankfully, these have a defined value: eight silver Spanish *reales*. A quarter-reale is a *cautorillo*—hardly worth a pirate's time—and the denominations ascend from there: *duro, escudito, escudo,* and *pistole*. Never expect to get your full money's worth when exchanging currencies in the Caribbean. The British colonies try to curtail the use of foreign monies and thus offer an atrocious exchange rate (all the more reason to smuggle and/or bury your loot).

Despite all the perplexity, there is one standard by which everyone from Jack Sparrow to Blackbeard measures any treasure: If it's shiny, take it.

CHAPTER FIVE

CHEATING DEATH

"Every soul has an appointment with death," Black-beard once said. "In my case, I happen to know the exact time.... It be foolish to battle fate, but I am pleased to cheat it." Cheating death, of course, is not something every man can do. It requires knowledge of a certain youth-spouting fountain.... Or the ability to escape seemingly inescapable situations. For example, Jack Sparrow's face-off with the kraken and subsequent return from Davy Jones's locker. Certainly, pitfalls and perils plague the life of a pirate, but these, although potentially mortal, can be prevented, thwarted, or squirmed out of entirely. Cheating death is much like any other form of cheating—and cheating, after all, is a method that pirates are sometimes forced to consider.

How to Escape from Being Tied Up

NEXT TO HIS SHIP, HIS TREASURE, AND HIS FINE WILY BRAIN, A PIRATE'S BEST FRIENDS ARE HIS HANDS. WITH THEM, HE CAN PINCH, FILCH, CLIMB, SWING, WIELD A CUTLASS, FIRE A FLINTLOCK, PLAY A JIG, OR SAVE HIS OWN SKIN. NOT SO WHEN THOSE HANDS ARE RESTRAINED. HAVING ONE'S HANDS TIED IS AN AFFRONT UN-THINKABLY CRUEL TO A PIRATE (ALTHOUGH PIRATES DO, AT TIMES, FIND IT NECESSARY TO TIE THE HANDS OF OTHERS—SUCH ARE THE IRONIES OF THE TRADE). WHEN SOME CRAVEN CUR FINDS IT AMUSING TO ROB YOU OF YOUR MANUAL DEXTERITY, AND THUS YOUR LIVELIHOOD, BY CON-STRAINING YOU AT THE WRISTS WITH HEMPEN ROPE AMID A CONDE-SCENDING CHUCKLE OF DOMINATION—AS ONCE HAPPENED TO JACK SPARROW AT THE HANDS OF THE AUTHORITIES AT PORT ROYAL—DON'T DESPAIR. WE'LL GET YOU OUT OF THIS BIND.

I. GO LIMP. When being apprehended by peacekeeper or ruffian—in the case of uniformed men like James Norrington and Cutler Beck-ett, what's the difference?—it's best to keep your wits about you. Take a deep breath. Relax. And, most of all, don't struggle while being tied up. Not only will doing so enrage your captor and provoke him to tighten your bonds to a brutal degree, it will constrict your muscles and tendons, which also makes for a tighter bond. Granted, the loss of personal freedom at the hands of barbaric dullards is difficult to ig-nore—not to mention that being tied up is usually a prelude to a punishment far more heinous (and permanent). Instead of despairing, think about how your captor will be bound by his own superiors once they learn of your swift escape, and take comfort in that small, poetic justice.

2. IT'S ALL IN THE WRISTS. Once nice and loose and limber, you'll be fit to be tied. It is of utmost importance to present your wrists to your captor in a specific way: Make two fists, hold them horizontally, extend them directly in front of you, and touch the sides of your wrists. Fortunately, that appears to be the most natural and normal way to have your hands tied, and it's also the easiest to escape from. What you should *not* do is put the heels of your palms together or cross your wrists; these positions will make the bonds much harder to squirm out of, not to mention potentially injurious while trying to do so.

3. GIVE 'EM THE SLIP. Now that you've been tied up and left alone, it's time to get wiggly with it. The gap between your wrists that was formed by the horizontal position of your fists should give you a precious bit of leeway. By twisting your wrists carefully and covertly sideways—careful of that rope; it's sure to be made of coarse hemp that can cause unseemly rope burn—you'll be able to free your wrists while appearing to remain constrained. You'll even be able to keep the rope from dropping to the floor, which you wouldn't be able to do if breaking it. In a way, this is a metaphor for Jack Sparrow's entire conduct. Why grunt and strain to break your bonds through brute force when you can employ some slippery cleverness? In any case, you probably aren't packing that much brute force anyway, so what choice do you have? Play to your strengths and live to play another day.

4. GET CREATIVE. You may not have the luxury of presenting your hands in such a way that a captor will unwittingly bind you the way you want to be bound; for instance, it's customary in some parts of so-called civilization to knock someone out before tying them up. If you wake to find yourself tightly bound, hogtied, or manacled by cold hard iron, it's time to break out the big guns. You'll likely have a guard of some sort, and that guard will likely be in possession of a dagger (or a key). If bribing the poor wretch with promises of untold riches doesn't work—cutting him in on your current scheme is a good proposition, albeit one you won't be honoring—you'll want to take the opposite tack. Taunt him. Insult his sister, his mother, his mother's sister, his dog, even his dentist. Anyone employed to guard a tied-up pirate can't be that much higher up socially than a pirate, and he's sure to be lower-classed and quick-tempered enough to take your bait. Once blinded by rage and ready to assault you, it's easy to bring down the underestimating dolt with a well-aimed kick to the ankles or a hard back-of-the-skull to the fellow's chin. The solution may not be the most elegant, but if it's the only way to get his knife and key, we're sure he'll understand someday.

Manacles present another problem entirely—but, as Jack Sparrow once discovered when shackled by Elizabeth Swann to the mast of the *Black Pearl*—a little well-placed oil from a shattered lantern can lubricate your hand enough to slip it through the iron. If the Kraken is at your back and hungry for pirate meat (see "The Kraken," page 165), that newfound liberation might not avail you much good. But at least you'll be able to go down with sword drawn and pride intact, hurling your defiance into the maw of death.

How to Fight a Tavern Full of Angry Men

BRAWLS—WHETHER ON A SHIP, IN THE STREET, OR AT A SEEDY TAVERN ON THE SALTIEST DOCKS IN THE CARIBBEAN—AREN'T NECESSARILY DEADLY. IN FACT, BEING ABLE TO SUCCESSFULLY SUFFER THE SLINGS AND ARROWS (AND FISTS AND KICKS) OF OUTRAGEOUS FORTUNE WILL MAKE YOU HARDIER (AND HARDER TO KILL). WE WON'T SPLIT HAIRS WHEN IT COMES TO THE CAUSE OF SUCH VIOLENT GOINGS-ON; WHEN FISTICUFFS BREAK OUT ANYWHERE NEAR A PIRATE, IT ALWAYS SEEMS TO BE THE PIRATE WHO GETS BLAMED. BUT ALL ABLE-BRAINED BUC-CANEERS MAKE A POINT OF AVOIDING FAMILIARITY WITH ANOTHER'S KNUCKLES. WHEN YOU'RE SWEPT UP IN A MELEE OF ANY KIND AGAINST YOUR WILL—ESPECIALLY THAT MOST COMMON OF ALL, THE TAVERN BRAWL—HERE'S WHAT TO DO TO KEEP YOUR SKIN INTACT, REMAIN ON TOP OF THE TUMULT, AND MAYBE EVEN COME OUT SMELLING LIKE (RUM-SOAKED) ROSES.

---

1. Cast off responsibility. Okay, time to be honest: Often a pirate is re-sponsible, at least indirectly, for a brawl. But we needn't let everyone know that. When some offending remark, gesture, action, or proposi-tion happens to ignite a certain indignity in another person—enough to wish to return the indignity in a physical fashion—the offended party has the momentum, both moral and physical. Before long, the whole crowd will get all ugly and moblike and turn against you. Be-

fore that can come to pass, divert the blame. It doesn't really matter whom you blame, as long as they're handy: the bartender, the sodden old sop beside you with his head buried in a rum pot, even your poor first mate (if he's handy and you've no one else to turn to). It is crucial, however, that your accusatory hue-and-cry is twice as loud and thrice as outraged as the person you offended. You don't have to be as grand a thespian as Jack Sparrow, who is often able to orchestrate entire battles while staying above the fray, but a little theatrics can go a long way. Before you know it, the person you originally enraged will be sputtering with frustration as the confused mass of brawlers winds up turning on themselves instead of on you.

2. SEEK THE EYE OF THE STORM. A ship caught in a hurricane fares far better by sailing directly for the calm eye of the storm than by trying to outpace and outmaneuver its destructive and capricious whims. Likewise, when caught in a brawl—especially of the raucous tavern variety—it's best to seek the center of the melee. It may seem counterintuitive, but amid the chaos you'll want to keep an eye on everything, including which way the tide of the battle is turning, just in case you find it prudent to throw in your lot with those who appear to be winning. Furthermore, the admittedly amateur and ad-hoc acrobatic skills you've picked up by climbing rigging and making daring escapes will come in handy: Swinging from chandeliers, dancing across tabletops, and climbing into the rafters are feats of nimbleness that not only honor the stylish, acrobatic tradition of Jack Sparrow but help you turn the force of the fight against itself.

YOU GOTTA DO WHAT YOU GOTTA DO

3. DIRTY IS JUST A WORD. Though the word *cheat* is open to interpretation, the fine art of the fistfight operates under its own code of decorum and conduct; an unspoken understanding exists among gentlemen when it comes to brawling, and fighting dirty is generally frowned upon. Well, let the gentlemen frown. As they observe good gamesmanship and a certain modicum of civility even in the face of flying fists, you'll be conscionably unencumbered and free to feign injury to acquire the upper hand, pretending to surrender in order to gain an escape route. Or, if you're unfortunate enough to become shackled, use those shackles to restrain a foe. As a last resort (or a first resort, if you prefer), deliver a well-timed knee to the nether regions.

A conscientious buccaneer uses every tool at his disposal—and if some swaggering dandy dares call you a dirty fighter for exercising your piratical prerogative, well, you have a knee or two with his name on it, too.

4.   ROLL WITH THE PUNCHES. It may be a wee bit of a stretch to call a pirate's reflex-sharpened agility "acrobatics." But by any name, there is a suppleness of posture and poise—call it slipperiness, if you will—that many pirates possess in spades, and Jack Sparrow more than most. Much of it has to do with the mindset of a pirate of Sparrow's acumen: Unlike stiff-upper-lipped seaman with their bluster and bombast, a pirate is much more apt to skulk, circumlocute, and sway with the tides—and in doing so offers less of a rigid target. The force of a blow to the head or belly is magnified greatly when leveled at a man who arrogantly stands his ground. But as anyone who's studied the Eastern martial arts knows, rolling with the punches makes those punches far less effective. Being relaxed also helps with the rolling. And a thimbleful of rum—or twelve, as Sparrow has been known to consume—definitely helps with the relaxing.

5.   JOG IT OFF. Discretion is the soul of self-preservation. In other words: You can't win every fight; and when you can't win, you run. Pirates as a whole don't like to admit when they're not up to a pugilistic challenge; even the sinuous Sparrow, himself a stealthy dodger of many a melee, has been known to nail the gizzards of poxy, cowardly crewmembers to his mast (metaphorically speaking, of course). Yet, there's a lot to be said for living to fight another

DEFLECT THE BLAME

GET OUT OF THE WAY

DON'T STICK AROUND

day—even if you're really just living to *avoid* fighting another day. It also bears mention that it takes a buccaneer a considerable amount of courage and intestinal fortitude to swallow one's rather bloated sense of pride—enough to run, hide, and leave one's enemies howling in vexation. In which case, your battle is all but won.

How to Treat a Wound

THE PRACTICE OF MEDICINE IS NOT HIGH ON A PIRATE'S LIST OF PRIORITIES. STILL, EVEN THE MOST HEADSTRONG AND FOOL-HARDY BUCCANEER KNOWS JUST HOW INDISPENSABLE A SHIP'S PHYSICIAN CAN BE. YET PIRATE SHIPS NEVER HAVE THEM. WHY WOULD A PIRATE OF CAPTAIN JACK SPARROW'S CALIBER (AND, AHEM, SOMETIMES LIMITED MEANS) WASTE PERFECTLY FINE LOOT TO KEEP A DOCTOR ON RETAINER WHEN YOU CAN JUST DO IT YOURSELF? OR, IF YOU'RE THE SQUEAMISH SORT, YOU CAN HAVE, SAY, A GUNNER OR DECKHAND TAKE CARE OF THE INJURED. EITHER WAY, PHYSICAL WOUNDS ARE AN UNAVOIDABLE UNPLEASANTRY IN A PIRATE'S LINE OF WORK, AND NO ADVENTURE IS TRULY SUCCESSFUL IF YOU HAVEN'T ACCRUED AT LEAST A FEW NICKS AND SCRAPES. HERE ARE A FEW WAYS TO HELP KEEP YOUR PIECES TOGETHER LONG ENOUGH TO GET TO A REAL (AND EXPENSIVE) PHYSICIAN.

I.   STOP THE BLEEDING. The most common types of wounds a pirate suffers are from blades, balls, and splinters (caused by large slivers of shrapnel that shoot around a ship's deck during cannon attacks). All remnants of the offending object must be removed, if possible, and direct pressure applied to the wound. Yes, that hurts. But bleeding out like a stuck pig hurts even worse. If pressure alone doesn't stanch the flow of blood, a tourniquet tied firmly above the wound should do the trick. Be careful that the tourniquet isn't too tight; if blood flow is cut off for too long, mortification may set in. And dead flesh means a dead patient, which kind of defeats the whole purpose.

2. CLEAN AND COVER. Have you ever seen a stab wound? Quite ugly. If for no other reason than to spare yourself the disgusting site of a crewman's gaping, gory gash, cover it up. But clean it first: A liberal dousing of whisky, rum, or gin should do the trick. Just make sure your patient, if conscious, is being held securely while the cleaning takes place; having alcohol poured into a large laceration is tantamount, pain-wise, to the original wound. Only it's worse, because you know it's coming. And when you do cover the wound, find the cleanest material available and wrap it firmly but not tightly around the offending area. Just try not to look at the ghastly damage while doing so.

3. INFECTION IS YOUR DIREST ENEMY. Pirates aren't exactly natural philosophers, but even the least scholastically inclined knows from experience that wounds tend to worsen. And worsen. And worsen. In fact, an untreated and unchecked injury can lead to infection or mortification—and that can lead to amputation. Peg-leg pirates may be a quaint stereotype, but it's hardly something a buccaneer aspires to. Can you imagine Jack Sparrow cavorting across Pelegosto footbridges and dueling on runaway water wheels with such a primitive prosthesis?

So, after a wound is cleaned and covered, keep it cleaned and covered. Don't peek at it and don't pick at it (that goes for both patient and "doctor"). The symptoms of infection include, well, a lot of really disgusting things we don't really want to get into here. Rest assured, you'll know it when you see (and smell) it. You don't want to go there.

4. GET TO A REAL DOCTOR. Yes, we know they're costly. Yes, we think they're quacks. But if you don't get your patient to a real doctor, their blood and guts and other foul stuff is on your hands. Not just metaphorically, but literally. So bite the bullet, go ashore, and seek professional treatment for serious wounds. After all, it's sound ship's policy; it could be *you* who's seriously wounded and in need of a trained physician or surgeon. And you wouldn't want your crew skimping on your medical care, would you? Jack Sparrow will be the first to tell you that no one should be in a hurry to send a crewmate to Davy Jones's Locker.

How to Stay Alive When Your Ship Sinks

THE OCEAN MAY BE AS FINE AS DRY LAND TO A PIRATE—AT LEAST IN A POETICAL SENSE. YET, NOT EVEN A PIRATE CAN WALK UPON THE WAVES. THAT'S WHY WE SAIL IN SHIPS. THEY FLOAT. BUT THE HARSH TRUTH IS, EVEN THE GRANDEST FRIGATE OR STURDIEST GALLEON IS BUT A FRAGILE EGGSHELL ADRIFT UPON THAT TEMPERAMENTAL LIQUID SKY WE CALL THE SEA (IF WE MAY WAX LYRICAL FOR A

1
APPLY A
TOURNIQUET

2
CLEAN THE
WOUND

3
COVER IT
UP

HOW TO TREAT A WOUND

MOMENT). BLUNTLY PUT: SHIPS SINK. THE THREAT IS EVEN MORE IM-
MINENT FOR A BUCCANEER. IN ADDITION TO THE TYPICAL TRAVAILS
THAT CONFRONT ALL MARITIME TRAVEL—SUCH AS WEATHER, OCEAN
CURRENTS, AND THOSE GREAT MYSTERIES OF THE DEEP (SEE "HOW TO
DEFEAT A SEA MONSTER," PAGE 146)—PIRATES MUST MAINTAIN THEIR
SHIP'S INTEGRITY IN THE FACE OF FELLOW RAIDERS, HOSTILE MARINES,
AND EVEN THE GROSS NEGLIGENCE OF A GROG-SOAKED BOATSWAIN. OC-
CASIONALLY, DESPITE THE TRUMPETED PROFICIENCY OF A BUCCANEER'S
SAILING ACUMEN, A PIRATE VESSEL DOES WIND UP AT THE BOTTOM OF
THE OCEAN. BUT ITS CREW, YOURSELF INCLUDED, DOESN'T HAVE TO GO
DOWN WITH THE SHIP.

1. JUMP SHIP. Maritime protocol demands that in times of peril where
   a sinking is imminent, a captain must go down with the ship. Well,
   standing on protocol is one thing; standing on water is another. Regardless of how or why your vessel is doomed, there's nothing noble
   about the captain—or any crewmember—staying onboard as the craft
   takes on water and descends into the depths. Technically speaking,
   you might not even stay *on* the ship as it sinks, even if you try: You'll
   be thrown into the ocean anyway because ships often rise, forecastle
   skyward, as water rushes into the breached hull, displacing air and re-
   distributing weight. An even worse scenario: A mast falls on you and
   cracks your skull while you're piously maintaining your tragic vigil.
   Sure, you'll wind up going down with the ship, but you won't be
   awake to enjoy it.

2. GET FLOATING. In a perfect sinking—if there were such a thing—there are plenty of lifeboats to go around. Everyone hops in, gets cozy, breaks out the dice and rum, and drifts away to the nearest island. But let's be real: The ocean is a harsh mistress, and pirate ships are none too concerned with such frivolous amenities as safety equipment and regulations. Life vests? Unheard of. Can you think of a less-dignified vision than that of Jack Sparrow or Hector Barbossa bobbing about the Caribbean in a puffy, bright-orange bib? Though it's *certainly* the way to go for civilians or seamen, a screaming neon flotation jacket presents a problem for a wanted criminal, if you get the drift.

Luckily, smaller boats are usually stowed aboard even the simplest pirate ship. Dinghies, tenders, pinnaces, dories, prams . . . there's bound to be a rowboat of some sort around. If that boat is in egregious disrepair—or there's simply no room after your fellow rats have piled in—you'll have to make do with whatever you can find. A flotation device can be made from almost anything wooden. Tables, doors, and even loose paneling can work in a pinch, and don't forget that your hold is likely full of empty barrels. A quick lashing of rope can turn them into a simple yet effective raft.

3. LEAVE THE LOOT. While searching for a suitable floatation device, you just may come across some of the booty you and your crew have amassed during your adventures. A bit of shine won't save you, though. Despite the temptation, don't try to stuff your pockets with loot before abandoning ship. (Food and water are allowable and probably even sensible, assuming such things are within easy reach and you don't get too grabby.) Not only will the extra weight drag you down and com-

plicate your maneuvering in the water, the extra time spent deliber-
ating over what to take and what to leave can make the difference between living and drowning. It won't be easy leaving behind those
great, glittering heaps of treasure, but when it's gone, it's gone. You can
always filch more. Remember: You can't take it with you, but if you
get too greedy, it will take *you* with *it*.

4.   AIM FOR SHORE. Sometimes fortune smiles on the wicked—and if
she chooses to do so on the day your ship sinks, you'll be in sight of
shore. Don't think, however, that you're as good as gold if you're within
eyeshot of dry land. If the tide is against you, your small boat or floatation device could just as readily be swept out into the open ocean as
wash up providentially on some sandy beach. You can row or paddle
toward your desired destination, but keep in mind that you will be
exhausted, dehydrated, hungry, maybe wounded, and perhaps even in
a mild state of shock and/or panic (although pirates should never
blanch at the prospect of navigating the sea in any capacity, even if,
deep inside, they're well beyond terrified). Sheer force of will alone
will not get you to shore if your limbs won't cooperate.

If Lady Luck is being pernicious, land will be nowhere in sight. That's
a bit trickier. Now is the time your experience and expertise as a sailor
will be indispensable: Using the sun, moon, stars, and your knowledge of
the currents, you must gauge the most likely direction in which to pro-
pel yourself. Being in the tropics helps; the North Star can usually be
found right on the horizon, and by holding it above a fixed point on
your raft—say, starboard for due west—you can steer in a roughly con-
sistent direction.

Heading for the nearest island might not be the most prudent course, if you know that island to be hundreds of leagues away. If you're certain land is nowhere at hand, it might be wiser to head for a nearby shipping lane. Even if a ship of the Royal Navy manned by the supercilious likes of James Norrington cruises by, and you're obviously a wet and bedraggled pirate floating on a piece of pine, they'll stop to rescue you, if for no other reason than to have the satisfaction of trying you for the high crime of piracy once you reach civilization. At that point, though, you'll need to quickly find and exploit an opportunity to escape. So try really, really hard not to let it get to that point—but remember that there is *no* escape from the hunger and thirst of the vast, unforgiving ocean.

5.   MAKE SIGNALS AND NOISE. Say you do wind up floating along in a shipping lane, and a magnificent galleon comes by, in all its resplendence. And then it passes you. And just keeps on going. Don't let your life depend on the presumed alertness and competence of others, especially if they may be of the dull, regimented mentality of the Royal Navy or merchant marines. Any dinghy worth its bulwarks should come equipped with a foghorn and a mirror. The breath-powered foghorn can carry much farther than a human voice across the waves, and the mirror can be used to reflect the sun and signal for help.

How to Survive Being Marooned

AROONING—THAT IS, THE DELIBERATE STRANDING OF A PERSON ON A REMOTE, UNINHABITED ISLAND—IS A PUNISHMENT RESERVED FOR ONLY THE MOST DESPICABLE PIRATE, ONE WHO DEFRAUDS OR MURDERS A FELLOW BUCCANEER. (ALTHOUGH THE HEINOUS, FEARSOME BLACKBEARD IS SAID TO HAVE MAROONED ALMOST HIS ENTIRE CREW TO KEEP A VAST HAUL OF PLUNDER FOR HIMSELF.) OF ALL THE TRIALS AND TRIBULATIONS A PIRATE CAN UNDERGO, BEING MAROONED IS THE SINGLE MOST TRAUMATIC. NOT ONLY IS YOUR PHYSICAL EXISTENCE AT STAKE, YOUR MIND AND SOUL ARE SUBJECT TO THE GREATEST EXTREMES OF ISOLATION, LONELINESS, AND HOPELESSNESS. BUT IF BEING A PIRATE WERE EASY, THEN EVERYONE IN THE CARIBBEAN WOULD BE ONE—SO ACCEPT THE RISK OF SOMEDAY BEING MAROONED, AND PREPARE YOURSELF ACCORDINGLY.

---

1. SEEK SHELTER. When the crew of the *Black Pearl* marooned their captain after the perfidious mutiny of Hector Barbossa, Sparrow is rumored to have gone mad from the heat—which may explain, in part, his rather, ah, *eccentric* personality traits. If you find yourself alone and ill-equipped on an island, the elements are your first and foremost enemy. Luckily, that part of the world provides well for its inhabitants, and building a hut from branches and grass—as well as pliable, fibrous, resilient palm fronds—should be no more difficult than mending a staysail.

    Don't overlook a gruesome yet more durable source of covering. Goats roam freely and wildly on many Caribbean isles, and goatskin—

besides housing the meat you need to live—can be cured in the sun and used as the framework of a hut (not to mention your body, should your clothes fall into disrepair). A tropical hut is no governor's mansion—it's not even a moderately appointed captain's quarters aboard a topsail schooner—but it will protect you from going loony in the glare of the sun.

2. FIND WATER. Water, water everywhere, and not a drop to drink. That lyrical adage (someone really should put it in a poem someday) becomes painfully resonant to a marooned pirate. As any sailor knows, drinking seawater—the most plentiful, life-giving liquid around—doesn't do a human any good. It may slake your thirst for a few seconds, but soon you'll feel more than a few ill effects. Seawater is three times saltier than blood, and even moderate consumption will lead to, ironically enough, rapid dehydration and increased thirst, followed by such unpleasant symptoms as muscle seizures, kidney failure, and brain damage (or worse). Not even one of Jack Sparrow's epic, rum-induced hangovers can compete.

The alternative is fresh water, and it's not as hard to find as you might think. Distillation—that is, boiling seawater and allowing the pure steam to condense on a piece of fabric, such as your shirt—is key. Coconut milk, though it takes work to access, will also help quench your thirst and keep you alive. (But don't drink too much of the milk undiluted—it will dehydrate you even more quickly than drinking none at all.) Leaves are also your friend: They can be used to capture steam and serve as collectors of dew or rainwater. As for drinking sweat or, well, other bodily fluids: We cannot recommend avoiding that measure highly enough. Even leaving aside the grossness factor, biological excretions are full of salt that will dehydrate you, just as seawater does.

3. STAY SOBER. It has been rumored, although not widely, that marooned pirates were sometimes left with a supply of alcohol. That may seem like a magnanimous, almost chivalrous gesture on the part of those marooning you, but don't be fooled. Drinking booze not only dehydrates, it impairs your faculties and judgment. Not only do you need to possess your full set of wits and reflexes, you must remain positive and focused. Alcohol has many other uses, including its antiseptic properties and flammability. Yes, we know it's tempting to get utterly besotted and sing your cares away before a bonfire on the beach. But do you really want to sit on that deserted beach for the rest of your very short, un-pirate-like life?

4. THINK: RAFT. If you're a pirate and a sound seafarer to boot, then just because you're marooned doesn't mean you don't know where you are. Your desperate, dehydrated mind may think that swimming for the nearest island is your best means of escape. Perish the thought. That's just the terror talking. Sharks, deadly currents, and exposure to elements are just a few of the perils you're sure to encounter while swimming even a short distance. Not to mention easily losing course and winding up in the middle of the open ocean.

    If, however, your situation becomes so dire that you feel you must submit to the whims and weather of the Caribbean, a raft is your safest option. Find the driest, lightest, largest pieces of wood and lay them on the ground. Cut notches into them. (You do have your trusty dagger, right? If not, then rig a rough blade out of your belt buckle.) Then, use woven plant fibers (strips of palm frond will do) to lash them together. Gather some fresh water, goat meat, and coconuts and stock up your new vessel, Captain! Just be careful—once you run out of those supplies and the raft comes apart at the seams a few days out, you'd better hope there's land or a ship on the horizon.

And one last word of advice: Despite the apocryphally poetic account of Jack Sparrow's daring escape from a deserted island, don't try crafting an ersatz raft by lashing together a couple of sea turtles. They'd probably find more dignity being made into soup.

5.   WHERE THERE'S SMOKE, THERE'S A SURVIVOR. As mentioned, the rich, sweet libation that is rum has a purpose beyond mere ingestion. As a flammable substance, it can be used as fuel to turn a bonfire into a rescue signal. While otherwise occupied building your raft, you should also build a fire (rubbing sticks together is common knowledge). Once it's burning, throw any rum you've been left with into the middle of the blaze. Granted, you're supposed to be avoiding the heat. But as Elizabeth Swann discovered while marooned with Jack Sparrow, a burning case of rum turns into a column of thick, dark smoke visible for dozens of miles in all directions. We can't all be as ingenious and self-sufficient as Captain Swann, but what worked for her can work for you.

6.   LIVING IS THE BEST REVENGE. When a pirate is being marooned, it's customary to give him a pistol—loaded with only a single shot. Obviously, you can't effectively hunt or defend yourself with a single ball;

the cruel motive behind such a gift is to give you an easy way out when the privations of the island are too much to bear. Don't take that way out. No matter how hungry, thirsty, sunburned, delirious, lonely, and, yes, frightened you become, never surrender.

We won't give you some lofty speech about the value of human life. Rather, we'll say this: If you don't live, you can't exact revenge. The person who put you on that island—say, Hector Barbossa—is still out there somewhere, sailing and singing and plundering away, and you simply can't let that pass. Furthermore, being marooned may serendipitously lead to finding a lost treasure or being rescued by someone who will sympathize with your ordeal—and provide the means to help you. Don't think of being marooned as a setback; think of it as a new if unexpected path toward your ultimate goal of riches, might, and infamy.

PIRATE WEAPONRY

1. Bandolier	4. Cutlass	7. Grenade
2. Blunderbuss	5. Dagger	8. Grappling hook
3. Cannon	6. Flintlock	9. Saber

PIRATE WEAPONRY

THE FINE ART OF BEING SOMEWHERE ELSE

No true, lionhearted pirate ever shirks from the likelihood of physical danger. But we can't state this enough: Why fight if you don't have to? Direct confrontation is almost philosophically repugnant to a pirate. In almost all circumstance, violent or not, placing yourself in the path of an opposing force accomplishes little in the way of personal, enlightened enrichment. True, every pirate is pretty much a walking, talking excuse for a crisis. But that doesn't mean you have to stick around and bear the brunt of the chaos when dangerous situations come to a head.

First of all, heed the warning signs. As a pirate, your mind—in truth, your very body—should be an instrument finely calibrated to detect the warning signs of imminent peril. Even while otherwise occupied, always keep an eye and an ear on the horizon. The sails of an enemy ship, the distant thunder of a cannonade, the yelp of distress in the street, the disciplined thud of marching boots, all can give you plenty of notice that a hostile entity is at your heels. We're not saying you did nothing to earn the wrath of such entities—be they military, piratical, or supernatural. But what's the use in letting them get the drop on you? Unless you're setting a deliberate, carefully designed trap, don't allow your enemies the benefit of confronting you directly.

Another point to keep in mind: the diversionary power of words. Never mind daggers, cutlasses, flintlocks, blunderbusses, and cannons; rhetoric is the true weapon of a pirate. Remember that the mind of a nonpirate is often cluttered with such flotsam as logic, morality, and propriety. Rhetoric is an effective way to derail these regimented intellectual methods. When accosted with an accusation, turn it back on the accuser. Or, better still, confess—but do so as if you were speaking of the weather, not some nefarious deed. Presenting such a confession free of all guilt—with a cheerful grin, even—is a paradox that can shut down a pursuer, even if it's just long enough for you to slip through his grasp. And though it may seem worse to have more than one pursuer after you, such a show of force can work to your benefit. Like a piece of raw meat thrown into a school of sharks, a bit of rhetorical speculation—for instance, "Does the *Black Pearl* really exist?"—can cause your enemies to argue and turn on one another. And when they're fighting among themselves, they're not paying attention to you.

Once your enemy has been sufficiently distracted, it's time to fade into the woodwork. Whatever you do, don't just turn tail and run. That will immediately get the hounds back on your trail, and your clever diversion will have been for naught. Instead, remain facing them, smiling and laughing (go ahead and mock them a little, if you like) as you slowly, imperceptibly begin to tiptoe backward. Preferably toward a door or a body of water that you can use as an exit. As long as they can still see your rugged visage out of the corner of their eye, they won't realize what you're up to until it's too late and you're on your way to freedom. Without, of course, having thrown a punch, or even an ill word.

THE LEGEND OF THE FOUNTAIN OF YOUTH

Cheating death is one thing. Beating it fair and square is another. For centuries, explorers and adventurers of all kinds have sought the Fountain of Youth, a mythic spring whose crystal waters are said to cure its bathers of that most widespread, hideous, untreatable, and terminal disease afflicting all humanity: growing old.

The exact location of the Fountain of Youth—indeed, its very existence—has been in doubt for as long as it's been rumored to exist. But Juan Ponce de León, a Spanish conquistador and onetime governor of Puerto Rico, heard tell of a whispered-about and magical Caribbean land that housed the fountain. A dip in its waters, the legend went, could cure all ailments, reverse and prevent the effects of aging, and imbue the imbiber with an enlightened and almost holy glow of body, mind, and spirit.

And so Ponce de León, having already become a man rich in material wealth, set off to search for the fabled fountain. He made numerous expeditions, none of which are reported to have yielded the mythic wellspring. In fact, many now claim that Ponce de León never searched for the fountain at all, and that the entire tale is a bit of apocrypha designed to add color to local legends.

That, of course, is exactly what Ponce de León would have wanted you to believe. Although history says he died in the sixteenth century from a poisoned arrow, who's to say that he isn't still alive somewhere today, sipping at the fountain and gloating over his conquest of the universe's greatest mystery?

One thing is certain: No pirate or adventurer in all the Caribbean has failed to be lured by the promise of the Fountain of Youth at one time in their adventures. Even Captains Jack Sparrow, Hector Barbossa, and Blackbeard were reputedly sucked into the search for the magical geyser, although it is only for legend to tell whether their quest ended with the prize of everlasting life.

MYSTERIES OF THE DEEP

So far we've explored the more mundane, though colorful, hurdles that a pirate must leap during the course of his exploits. But the ocean holds far greater and stranger threats than deserted islands or the Royal Navy. Vaster than the imagination, the Caribbean contains wonders and horrors that the human mind can scarcely perceive. But pirates are no ordinary humans. Leading an existence so disassociated from humdrum, everyday reality makes them susceptible to the sea's more supernatural elements—everything from curses and monsters to mermaids and magical treasures. Just because pirates are more open to the existence of such phantasmagoria doesn't mean they know how to deal with it. Below are a few admittedly meager suggestions and guidelines that may help with that most esoteric of piratical pursuits: knowing the unknowable.

How to Defeat a Sea Monster

BY AND LARGE, THE VERY ACT OF THINKING YOU'RE ABLE TO DE-
FEAT A SEA MONSTER IS ENOUGH TO GET YOU CONSIGNED TO A
LUNATIC ASYLUM. IN THE CARIBBEAN, AT LEAST, THE TERM SEA
MONSTER IS SYNONYMOUS WITH DAVY JONES'S PET, THE MIGHTY AND
MALEVOLENT KRAKEN (SEE "THE KRAKEN," PAGE 165), AND THERE'S NO
MORE FEARSOME BEING THAT EXISTS IN ALL OF PIRATEDOM. JONES IS RU-
MORED TO HAVE KILLED THE CREATURE—BUT WHEN IT COMES TO THE
SUPERNATURAL, YOU NEVER KNOW WHAT MIGHT BE RESURRECTED OR
REINCARNATED. AND, WITHOUT A DOUBT, THE OCEAN IS FAR TOO VAST AND
DEEP FOR THERE TO BE ONLY ONE SUCH LEVIATHAN LURKING WITHIN. IF
YOU HAPPEN TO BUMP INTO A SEA MONSTER, YOUR CHANCES OF SURVIV-
ING ITS BLOODTHIRSTY RAMPAGE ARE PRETTY LOW, BUT THESE TIPS WILL
HELP BETTER YOUR CHANCES. AFTER ALL, AS THE KRAKEN FINALLY
LEARNED, EVEN THE MOST NIGHTMARISH BEHEMOTH CAN HAVE A BAD DAY.
AND A BAD DAY FOR A SEA MONSTER IS A GOOD DAY FOR YOU.

1. DON'T PANIC. If you think your ship has hit a reef but you're in the
    open ocean, it's probably a sea monster. Stay calm. Whatever you do,
    don't flop around like a flounder with its head cut off. The survival of
    you and your crew now depends on operating as a team and defend-
    ing yourselves in a disciplined, coordinated way. If a sea monster is in-
    deed knocking on your hull and asking to come in, you have, at best,
    minutes to act—so collect yourself and use that time wisely.

    You needn't be as suicidally nonchalant as Jack Sparrow, who famously greeted the slavering Kraken with a hearty "Hello, Beastie!" upon confronting the creature face-to-face (or face-to-gaping-maw-of-hell, as the case may be). But try to maintain a modicum of decorum. Look at things philosophically. If you're doomed anyway, why give the poor creature indigestion?

2.   CANNONBALLS MAKE GREAT APPETIZERS. Let's assume that you're not ready to go down the monster's gullet without a fight. Once your crew is sufficiently cool and collected to coordinate an attack, you'll need to orchestrate a massive and surgically targeted cannonade. The sea monster will likely use tentacles, jaws, or some combination of the two to begin assaulting your ship. As soon as it reveals itself, give the order to fire; individual cannon shots will inflict nothing more than cosmetic harm, so be sure to maximize impact by concentrating all your fire on a single spot. The monster should soon withdraw in pain and dismay and cease hostilities. But don't be fooled: Despite evidence to the contrary, the creature is likely not dead, just dazed and perhaps a bit offended. But you've bought yourself some time.

3.   GET EXPLOSIVE. While your cannonade is giving its short, sharp shock, gather your stores of gunpowder and bring them above deck. And that's not all: As much as it may pain you to part with them, all barrels of rum or other liquor must be mixed with the gunpowder. As soon as the monster rears its head (or fins or scales or tentacles or what-have-you), capitalize on the momentum of your first strike by dropping these volatile barrels, rum and gunpowder in a merry mix, on the resurfaced creature. Then, while the barrels are falling, the can-

FOCUS ALL YOUR FIRE ON ONE SPOT

niest shot in your crew must put a musket ball into one of the barrels. That's all it should take: When one barrel explodes, it will ignite the next, and on and on. This chain reaction—in addition to the walloping of cannonballs previously delivered—might just be enough to scare the thing off. Or you might just make it angrier.

4. GIVE IT WHAT IT WANTS. Though certainly a few freelance sea monsters roam the Caribbean, sinking ships and eating crews for the sheer hijinks of it all, many more—like the Kraken—work for someone. The Kraken were in the evil employ of Davy Jones, and who's to say Jones doesn't command an entire fleet of such behemoths? In which case, it's highly likely that a sea monster is attacking you for a specific reason: They want something—or some*one*—on your ship. Immediately, order every crewmember to be searched for the Black Spot, that inky and nefarious blemish that mars the skin of one who owes his soul to Davy Jones. And if you find a person with such a mark, you must then decide whether to cast him (or her) off in a dinghy, thus drawing away the ire of Jones's monstrous agent. It's a mercenary move, and one that will haunt you forever. Sometimes, though, being a pirate is about making the tough decisions.

How to Vanquish Davy Jones

I AM THE SEA," DAVY JONES IS KNOWN TO BOAST. ACCORDINGLY, OF ALL THE BEINGS (HUMAN OR OTHERWISE) THAT INHABIT THE CARIBBEAN, NONE CAN SINK A PIRATE'S HEART FASTER THAN HE. CAPTAIN OF THE GHOSTLY FLYING DUTCHMAN AND THE DOOMED FORMER LOVER OF THE GODDESS CALYPSO (SEE "CALYPSO," PAGE 164), JONES IS AN IMMORTAL MONSTER DRIVEN BY A BROKEN HEART AS MUCH AS A THIRST FOR CRUELTY AND DESTRUCTION. HE'S ALSO NOT EXACTLY WHAT YOU'D CALL PRETTY; IN FACT, THE SIGHT OF HIS TENTACLED VISAGE—EVEN THE MERE MENTION OF HIS NAME—HAS CAUSED THE MOST BARNACLE-CRUSTED BUCCANEER TO WAIL LIKE A FLEDGLING PELICAN. JONES'S PRIMARY WEAKNESS IS THAT HE CAN WALK ON DRY LAND ONLY ONCE EVERY TEN YEARS, BUT THAT'S SCANT COMFORT TO A SALTY, SEA-DWELLING PIRATE. TRUE, JONES DOES FUEL THE DUTCHMAN WITH THE SOULS, SWEAT, AND TEARS OF THE CURSED AND THE DAMNED. BUT THAT DOESN'T MEAN YOU HAVE TO BECOME ONE OF THEM.

---

1. ROLL THE DICE. We may have previously warned you against dicing with Davy Jones. We still do. But if you have no other choice, the fact is that Jones is a gambling man-thing, and he can sometimes be persuaded—as Will Turner once did—to play a game of Liar's Dice. The higher the stakes, the more tempted he becomes. If you're captured and conscripted to serve a hundred years on the *Flying Dutchman*, you may be able to convince him to grant you parole, if you agree to collect, say, a hundred fresh souls to man his crew. Once free of the *Dutch-*

man, you can begin plotting a more permanent solution. If Jones has a fault, it's overconfidence. He believes it inconceivable that one of his lowly minions might eventually be his downfall. Play the part of the desperate, terrified lackey and use his megalomania to your advantage. Play your dice right, and you may even gain immortality of your own. (Oh, and one more thing: Make sure you're actually good at Liar's Dice. The one thing you *don't* want to do is bet against Davy Jones and lose.)

2. SUMMON CALYPSO. Before Davy Jones became the creepy, organ-playing, soul-stealing, ship-sinking, Kraken-commanding, crab-clawed, octopus-faced monstrosity that he is today, he was a human being.

CONSULT AN EXPERT IN OCEAN MAGIC

Enough of his humanity remained to allow him to fall in love with Calypso, the ocean goddess who entrusted him with the task of ferrying those who die at sea to the afterworld. Summoning Calypso is a sure way to stop Jones dead in his tracks, although it's hard to gauge whether her appearance will enrage the sinister captain or render him a whimpering, lovelorn wretch. Either way, you've broken through some of his defenses and bought yourself some time. And it's not like Calypso is that hard to find—she was condemned by the Brethren Court to take the mortal form of the Obeah priestess Tia Dalma.

3. STEAL HIS HEART. Literally. As Jack Sparrow and others have come to discover, Davy Jones keeps his heart in the Dead Man's Chest, along with his tearstained love letters to Calypso. Swords do not harm him—he'll laugh as you impale him with your cutlass and simply keep on fighting—but his heart is of particular vulnerability. Finding the Dead Man's Chest aboard the *Flying Dutchman* and then obtaining the key won't be a day with the dolphins, but with a little luck and some ingenuity—not to mention the successful application of steps 1 and 2, above—you may just have a chance to sink a blade into the dastard's vile, insidious heart. There is a drawback to vanquishing Jones, however: You must take his place as captain of the *Flying Dutchman* and ferryman of the dead. On the bright side, you always wanted your own ship, right?

NOT AS HEARTLESS AS HE LOOKS

How to Cope with Mermaids

NOT ALL CREATURES OF THE SEA ARE HIDEOUS MONSTERS LIKE THE KRAKEN. SOME CAN BE QUITE FETCHING, IF A COMELY WOMAN WHO HAPPENS TO BE PART HUMAN AND PART FISH IS YOUR IDEAL OF BEAUTY. BUT THERE'S A DIABOLICAL HEART BEATING BENEATH THOSE RAVISHING SCALES. BE WARY IN DEALING WITH THAT FAIR RACE, REGARDLESS HOW LONG YOU'VE BEEN AT SEA AND WITHOUT FEMALE COMPANIONSHIP.

1.   THEY'RE OUT THERE. Mermaids may seem like rare beings, if you don't consider them mythical altogether. The truth, however, is that mermaids have been represented in the artwork, stories, and religions of civilizations throughout time. That didn't happen by accident. Where there are humans—and water—there are mermaids. Don't blindly assume that you'll never run across such a seldom-seen creature. Prepare yourself. After all, a lot of people have never seen a pirate as exotic and inscrutable as Jack Sparrow—but that doesn't make *him* any less real. Or less dangerous.

2.   CHARMS MEAN HARM. A mermaid's most alluring attribute is also her deadliest: her sheer, overwhelming, irresistible charm. You might think that an inhabitant of the deep sea would hold little romantic appeal for a man born on land—but you, my friend, have never seen one in the flesh. It's part of a mermaid's magic to be able to bewitch and be-

wilder the target of her affections—and the exoticness of her form heightens, not lessens, that magic. It doesn't even matter what your gender or natural inclinations are; a mermaid can cloud your mind with desire and lure you into betrayal, and a watery grave. Don't give her the chance. At the first site of one, you have approximately half a moment to turn and run before your soul is hers. We recommend you use that half a moment in the wise execution of a hasty retreat.

3. SWIM AT YOUR OWN RISK. Rumors abound that a key ingredient in the Fountain of Youth ritual is the tear of a crying mermaid. For this reason, some longevity-pursuing pirates may be tempted to hunt these ladies of the deep. But mermaids aren't exactly the catch of the day. And if you come face to face with one, you may find your-self falling hook, line, and sinker for her charms. Just ask Philip about his first encounter with Syrena.

How to Break a Curse

YOU MAY BE STARTING TO DISCERN A PATTERN HERE: PIRATES AND MAGIC DON'T USUALLY MIX. SOMETIMES MAGIC FINDS YOU, HOWEVER, AND THAT'S NOT OFTEN A GOOD THING. THE CARIBBEAN'S RICH TRADITION OF MAGIC AND MYSTICISM HAS A FLIPSIDE, AND THAT FLIPSIDE IS THE CURSE. GRANTED, CURSING OF THE MILDER AND MUNDANE VARIETY IS PART OF A PIRATE'S PATOIS. BUT REAL CURSES—THE ONES THAT RENDER YOU BLIND OR BALD OR TRANSFORMED INTO A FROG— ARE FRIGHTENINGLY COMMON THROUGHOUT PIRATEDOM. IT'S NOT HARD

TO SEE WHY: PIRATES BY NATURE ARE ALWAYS STICKING THEIR NOSES INTO OTHER PEOPLE'S TREASURE, AND WHAT BETTER WAY TO GUARD TREASURE THAN WITH A CURSE? SO IF YOU DO FIND YOURSELF SUPERNATURALLY STRICKEN, DON'T DESPAIR. EXERCISE THESE OPTIONS.

1.   GET YOUR BEARINGS. The first step in any diagnosis, supernatural or otherwise, is to locate the source of the affliction. Assuming you haven't been stricken with leprosy or madness or some other curse that renders your piratical abilities impaired—in which case, have fun in the colony/asylum; we'll send postcards—you need to determine exactly when, where, and how you became cursed. It shouldn't be hard. What was the last big plunder you undertook? What was taken? Is there a legend surrounding it? Are there locals, particularly of the mystical variety, who can fill you in on the details? Remember, curses don't happen without reason. There's a direct cause and effect at play, such as in the harrowing example of the crew of the *Black Pearl*, who were doomed to live forever as insatiable, eternally thirsty skeletons after stealing a cache of enchanted Aztec gold. Find out who or what you've angered, and you're halfway there.

2.   CORRECT YOUR COURSE. Now that you've discovered the person or entity behind your curse, it's time to do something about it. Don't dally with evasion or countercurses. You're in deep enough water as it is. Bite the musket ball, take responsibility, and take the necessary steps to *un*-anger the offended party—even if, as Hector Barbossa and the

Black Pearl crew found out, that entails returning all your booty, plus the blood of each perpetrator on your ship. You don't have to believe you've done anything wrong (although you more than likely did). But contrition and reparation may be the only way to get your old life, and your old flesh, back.

3. NIP THE CURSE IN THE BUD. An ounce of prevention is worth a pound of cure—and that goes double when it comes to curses. Being a pirate means making your own rules, but there is a limit; when planning your marauding exploits, it's best to stick with the tried, true, and known sources of booty. If you're unsure exactly whom you're plundering—but you do know that there are signs of magic everywhere, and that other pirates avoid the area like the blight— stop and think. Is it worth the risk? Remember that you may end up having to return all the treasure, and some blood besides, just to escape with your skin and sanity intact. Don't let greed overwhelm you. Booty is just a means to an end—that end being freedom. And the undead crew of the *Black Pearl* is semiliving proof that freedom is something no cursed pirate is privy to.

TOP TEN PIRATE SUPERSTITIONS

Treading the brackish water between the natural and the supernatural, pirates are a superstitious lot. After all, most pirates have witnessed firsthand all manner of magic artifact, arcane creature, and otherworldly being. In a way, a buccaneer's belief in superstitions is only sensible. That doesn't mean that all superstitious views and practices are anything more than utter poppycock. But, in the absences of organized religion, an understanding of the basics of the Brethren's superstitions is, in a way, a window into the pirate's soul. A smudged and grimy and rather opaque window, but a window nonetheless.

1. KEEP CATS. Of all a pirate's various superstitions, the keeping of cats aboard ship is perhaps the most sensible and humane. After all, the parallel between Jack Sparrow and your average feline are numerous and undeniable: Both are discriminatingly social yet ultimately solitary creatures, and both predicate their existence on being agile, adaptable, stealthy, wily, and difficult to kill—not to mention that each possesses a certain perverse charisma that can be simultaneously repugnant and irresistible. Black cats would seem to be the feline variety pirates would most identify with, and, indeed, they are considered good luck on a pirate ship (despite being considered bad luck just about everywhere else). Well-kept, well-fed cats are considered a protection against harm, and the casting of a cat overboard is sure to bring bad weather and calamity. Cats with extra toes—that is, polydactyl cats—are even luckier. This superstition may have arisen for a practical purpose: Cats catch rats, and rats abound on ships.

Especially those whose crew have rather lassez-faire attitudes toward hygiene. In that sense, a cat's cleanliness is perhaps where the animal's nature diverges most notably from that of the pirate.

2. SAVED BY THE BELL. From friendly foghorns to the ominous horns of a vaporing buccaneer, sounds are potent signals in the world of the pirate. A ship's bell carries a special significance. To a real degree it is considered the heartbeat of a vessel, and its ringing by a crewmember can be used as a warning, a celebration, an affirmation, and, of course, a peal of good luck. Its song is believed to ward away danger and evil spirits, although a bell that rings itself portends the presence of evil aboard. Granted, detractors of Jack Sparrow might say that *he* is the evil aboard. But we don't listen to such claptrap, do we?

3. RIGHT FOOT FIRST. Despite the pirate's savage reputation, there is a method to his madness. Among the many articles of protocol that govern the boarding of a ship for the purpose of plunder, there are bound to be superstitions—and the most widespread is the belief that misfortune will surely come to a buccaneer whose first step on a soon-to-be-looted ship is made with his left foot. The superstition may be rooted in the same distrust many people, pirates and otherwise, have of left-handed people. Which is, of course, wholly irrational. Then again, we're pirates, not logisticians. In any case, when properly soused, Sparrow doesn't bother to distinguish between right foot and left, and he seems to have done quite well for himself.

4. WHISTLES AND SNEEZES. A pirate vessel lives and dies by the wind—and naturally such a capricious, quick-tempered force is accorded a certain amount of personification. Picture, as the pirate does, an elemental being whose puffed cheeks can blow either gentle, fortuitous breezes or the deadliest of hurricanes. Superstitious buccaneers believe that this creature is easily offended—and that a pirate's whistling and sneezing can be taken by the mighty wind as a form of mocking. Such actions are frowned upon, therefore, lest the ridiculed wind-god retaliate by whistling or sneezing your ship into oblivion. If you scoff at the idea of such superstitious nonsense, remember that the Kraken also sneezes, and there's nothing symbolic or personified about that beastie.

5. DOFF TO THE DEAD. As gruesome as it is to contemplate, the so-called civilized authorities of the Caribbean colonies often saw fit to display the corpses of condemned and executed pirates in the harbors where they were hanged. Yes, it gives us a chill, too. Though it may be merely a personal idiosyncrasy on the part of Captain Jack Sparrow, his practice of doffing his hat and silently holding it to his chest as he passes these poor, dangling Brethren may be more than simple superstition. Certainly, it invites a similar fate to oneself *not* to show such solemn tribute. But there's also a true reverence in such a gesture, one that reminds a pirate that, despite differences and self-interest, fraternity and empathy can and should be at least a small component of the pirate life.

6. THE NAME REMAINS. Although it may be opportune at points in a pirate's life to assume another name and identity—even the proud

Sparrow felt the need to occasionally go by the alias "Mr. Smith"—most pirates consider their *ships* a different matter. Generally, a ship once christened stays so; the renaming ceremonies required by tradition are elaborate and taxing. Sparrow, as usual, was an exception: His ship, originally named the *Wicked Wench*, went down in flames before being resurrected, charred and black, by Davy Jones. Given the circumstance, rechristening it the *Black Pearl* seemed wholly appropriate.

7. BURY THE DEAD. Just as the keeping of cats while at sea has a practical basis, so does the superstition that the dead may not rest aboard a ship. Corpses tend to stink up the place, and a ship is a place of close quarters with little hygiene or ventilation. Besides, a dead body is a constant reminder of—and one might say a magnet for—death itself, which perpetually dogs a pirate's heels. A proper, respectful burial at sea, even if done in extreme haste, is one way to appease Davy Jones and keep death at bearth for another day.

8. SILVER AND GOLD. Precious metals and coin are always welcome on a pirate ship. In truth, that's sort of the whole idea. But it brings greater luck—and greater reward—to a ship that's been built with a silver coin under the mast and a gold coin in the keel. Riches attract riches, and the small sacrifice of these coins helps ensure smooth sailing, calm waters, and felicitous winds. Just don't let any skinflint in your crew get the idea of trying to dig the coins out of the wood. Once removed, the coins won't be able to buy your way out of the bad luck you've brought on yourself.

9. WHITHER WOMEN? As we've already touched upon, piratedom—while progressive in many ways—is sometimes a bit regressive when it comes to the great egalitarian spirit its members are supposed to possess. Where ships' figureheads are considered lucky if carved in the shape of a woman, actual women on a ship are considered, by a small percentage of pirates, to be bad luck. For once and for all, let's quash and quell such nonsense. Angelica is just one of the many female pirates who have more than proved their mettle, as if they need to prove anything to anyone. The only advice we can give to the aspiring pirate who may so happen to be of the female gender is this: If some primitive, backward-thinking cad won't let you enlist on his ship, just get your own and captain it yourself. You'll doubtlessly do a better job. And a fairer one.

10. PAT, SPIN, SPIT. Like Jack Sparrow's peculiar yet reverent doffing of the cap in the presence of hanged pirates, other buccaneers practice their own odd and individual superstitions. For instance, when Joshamee Gibbs and the duo of Pintel and Ragetti first saw Sparrow's Black Spot, they instinctively performed a small ritual: They patted the pockets of their shirts, spun around in a circle, and spat on the ground. Presumably this was meant to ward off the presence of Davy Jones and keep the Spot from rubbing onto them. Or the three pirates may simply have been just a wee bit rum-soaked. Either way, it probably wouldn't hurt.

THE PIRATE PANTHEON

With one foot in the muck of the real world and the other in the un-knowable beyond, pirates hold a unique place. They're constantly surrounded by beings that transcend mortality and reality, as well as magic artifacts that reflect their terrifying power. But you're not afraid, are you? Pirates scoff at the thought of the supernatural even while secretly respecting it—and much of that respect comes from knowledge. Learn about the pantheon of gods and monsters that inhabit the Caribbean and you'll be far better equipped to conduct yourself in a nonplussed, even unimpressed fashion when they rear up and confront you throughout the course of your adventures. In spite of the heat, humidity, hoards, and horrors, always remember the ultimate and defining maxim of the pirate: Never let them see you sweat.

THE BLACK SPOT. Blights and blemishes are nothing new to a pirate. It's not like you can be bothered to bathe beyond the occasional dip in the drink, and a kiss of scurvy around the gills is considered a sign of distinction in some pirate quarters. Tattoos (as well as scarred brands courtesy of the East India Trading Company) are numerous among the buccaneer populace. One mark, however, is never welcome on the skin of a sea rover: the Black Spot. When placed on the body of a pirate by Davy Jones, this blemish of deathly ebony can't be scrubbed off. (That's assuming a pirate would even know where to find some soap.) Even worse: It calls the raven-ous Kraken to the one who is Spotted, thus ensuring the poor soul does Jones's bidding always. It's rumored that the few intrepid pirates who have managed to lose the Spot and live have suddenly become conscientious about washing themselves—particularly their fore-arms—on a regular basis.

CALYPSO. The Caribbean hath no fury like a goddess scorned—and Calypso is proof. Her romance with Davy Jones is as convoluted as it is tragic, but their entangled hearts wound up splitting forever after they each betrayed the other; Jones, it is said, was behind the Brethren Court's binding of the goddess into the human form Tia Dalma, an Obeah priestess. She was finally freed of the mortal shell, but her spirit remains in the Caribbean breezes and on its waves, al-though she is still not a being to be trifled with. Possessing formi-dable powers that include creating great, ship-smashing maelstroms and the ability to resurrect the dead (as she did for Hector Barbossa), Calypso should be respected and feared. But mostly feared.

THE DEAD MAN'S CHEST. Hiding one's heart away may make sense in a purely symbolic way, but Davy Jones is not a creature of such sub-tlety. When he was scorned by his love Calypso after a decade of di-abolical service to her, Jones carved out his own heart and locked it in the Dead Man's Chest. And then he buried it so that none, him-self included, may ever hurt it again. That plan, of course, was thrown out the porthole when Jack Sparrow hunted down the chest, stole the key from Jones, and abducted the monster's heart to free himself of his own service to Jones. It was later acquired by James Norrington and ultimately caused a great battle between him, Jones,

Sparrow, and Will Turner. Turner's own heart wound up in the chest, which is now safely kept by his wife, Captain Elizabeth Swann.

THE KRAKEN. The duo of Pintel and Ragetti may not be able to settle on the proper pronunciation of "Kraken," but that is of no consequence. A simple, bloodcurdling scream will do. Massive, monstrous, and malevolent, the oddly squidlike and coldly intelligent beast has an appetite the size of the Caribbean itself. And its favorite meal is pirates, especially those marked with the dreaded Black Spot. That said, the Kraken isn't picky. It's more than happy to aim its Herculean tentacles, face-erasing suckers, razor-sharp teeth, and slimy spittle at any human foolish enough to cross its path. And even those who miraculously survive its wrath are scarred for life, both physically and mentally. Ragetti may have testily told Pintel, "It's a mythological creature, I can calls it what I wants!"—but when all is said and done, the Kraken speaks for itself.

JACK SPARROW'S COMPASS. To lapse into the meandering current of philosophy for a moment: A pirate is nothing without a direction in life. Jack Sparrow, as much of a scoundrel and scallywag as he appears, is a pirate with a higher purpose. Whether it's the pursuit of wealth, women, or immortality, Sparrow knows what he wants, and he knows how to get it. Or at least he knows how to stagger and swagger toward it with one eye open and a quip on his tongue. And although his moral compass may be slightly malfunctioning, his true compass—the one given to him by Calypso while in the guise of Tia Dalma—works quite well. Others may assume it to be broken because its needle doesn't point due north. That's because it's a magical device that points in an entirely different direction: the source of the holder's greatest and most deeply felt desire. Sparrow has used this compass to locate everything from treasure to safety to, well, a bottle of rum, and it's alleged that he's currently using it to pursue the most valuable and powerful thing in all the world: the Fountain of Youth. Logic, of course, dictates that the compass is worthless if you don't have unshakably strong, clearly defined desires—not to mention the burning passion to pursue those desires to the ends of the earth. And in that department, Jack Sparrow is never, ever lacking.

Appendix: Piratical Lingo

AFT: The direction pointing back toward the rear of a ship or boat.

AHOY: A greeting used by pirates and other sailors to call from one seagoing vessel to another.

ALE: A popular drink for pirates while in port; it was rarer than rum on-board ship, because of its tendency to go bad.

ALOFT: Place description for anything or anyone found in the rigging.

AMIDSHIP: Generally, anything in the vicinity of the center of the ship; technically, the precise midpoint between fore and aft structural lines.

ARTICLES: The written code of conduct for any given pirate ship; every crewmember must swear to abide by these rules.

AVAST: A pirate's command meaning a simple *stop*, an irritated *cut it out*, or a determined *cease and desist*, depending on the tone of delivery.

BALLAST: Heavy weights carried by a ship to achieve proper balance for sailing, particularly when not carrying a full cargo.

BARQUE: Generally, any small sailing ship; technically, a ship with at least three masts arranged in one of several configurations.

BELAY: To make a rope secure by wrapping it around some form of support fitting. Also used colloquially to mean *stop*.

BILGE: The lowermost inside part of a ship's hull, between the lowest deck and the bottom. Water that collects here is *bilgewater*, which itself is sometimes called *bilge*.

BLIMEY: A working-class British exclamation of surprise or irritation; e.g., *Blimey, Jack doesn't know which way we're going.*

BLUNDERBUSS: A short, wide-barreled musket with a flaring muzzle; a favorite pirate weapon, it sprays shot in a broad pattern.

BOATSWAIN: The ship's officer with responsibility over the rigging, anchors, and other similar equipment. Pronounced (and sometimes spelled) *bos'n* or *bosun*.

BOUNTY: A reward offered by the authorities for the successful capture of a wanted pirate.

BOW: Generally, the front of any ship; more specifically, the frontmost oar or oarsman on any boat being rowed. Pronounced *bough*, not *bo*.

BOWSPRIT: A thick support pole extending from a ship's bow, to which the rigging is fastened as far forward as possible.

BRIG: The jail onboard a pirate ship or any ship. The word *brig* is also used as an abbreviation for brigantine (see below).

BRIGANTINE: A sailing ship with two masts, both rigged square (i.e., with the sails mounted on spars perpendicular to the mast).

BROADSIDE: Generally, the entire side of a ship's hull; more specifically, the full array of weaponry fired from one side of a ship.

BUCKO: Term of casual direct address to a man suggesting that he is something between a friend and an enemy; e.g., *Listen, bucko, put down that gun.*

BULKHEAD: Any vertical partition onboard acting as a wall to provide structural support and divide a ship's interior into different compartments.

CAREEN: To tilt a ship to one side, whether merely leaning while under sail or turned all the way onto its side for repairs on land.

CARIBBEAN: Having to do with the Caribbean Sea, which lies between North and South America and is named for the native Carib people who lived on its shores.

CHAIN SHOT: Two cannonballs or half-cannonballs joined by a chain; fired at an enemy ship to destroy its rigging.

CLAP OF THUNDER: Slang for a strong alcoholic drink, such as a triple-strength tankard of grog.

COFFER: A secure box, often watertight, for storing a ship's treasury; a ship's "official" treasure chest.

COLORS: Colloquial term for a pirate flag; e.g., *Hoist the colors!* Frequently used with British spelling: *colours.*

CORSAIR: Generally, a pirate ship built and rigged for speed; specifically, one such operating along the Barbary Coast with government sanction.

COXSWAIN: The officer who commands one of a ship's smaller rowboats while boarding, ferrying the captain to shore, etc. Pronounced *cox'n.*

CROW'S NEST: The lookout platform high on a ship's mast, where an attentive pirate keeps watch for other ships and for land.

CUTLASS: A curved, short, heavy, single-edged sword or machete; the preferred combat blade of Caribbean pirates because of its efficiency in close quarters.

DAGGER: Any small hand knife carried for use as a weapon; a pirate's weapon of last resort when enemies have engaged at hand-to-hand range.

FATHOM: A measurement of ocean depth equal to six feet (1.83 meters).

FLINTLOCK: A gun whose gunpowder is ignited by a spark from a small piece of flint (hard quartz) attached to the hammer.

FLOG: To beat with a whip or stick; this was a traditional form of discipline for pirates as well as naval seamen prior to the 20th century.

FORE: Generally, toward the front of a ship; more specifically, pertaining to the rigging around a ship's frontmost mast.

FORE AND AFT: Literally a reference to the front and back of a seagoing vessel, this expression is used to mean "along the entirety of the ship."

FORECASTLE: The section in the front of a ship that encompasses crew quarters as well as storage rooms for equipment, food, etc. Pronounced (and sometimes spelled) *fo'c'sle.*

FREEBOARD: The space between a ship's uppermost deck and the water line.

GALLEON: A large sailing ship with at least three masts; a Spanish ship design first dating from the 15th century.

GANGPLANK: A ramp used as a portable bridge from ship to dock. Extended over the open sea in the legendary method of pirate execution: *walking the plank*.

GRAPE SHOT: A loose mass of metal slugs, rocks, glass shards, etc., fired from a cannon to spray short-range destruction over a broad area.

GRAPPLE OR GRAPPLING IRON: A multipronged hook at the end of a rope used to seize hold of an enemy ship in order to board it.

GRENADOE: A hollow, grapefruit-size iron ball filled with gunpowder and shrapnel, lit with a fuse, and fired from a hand cannon.

GROG: Rum diluted with water; the most common alcoholic drink of pirates, since rum (which doesn't spoil) could be added to stale water to hide the rancid taste.

GUNWALE: The top plank along the edge of a ship or boat's hull. Pronounced (and sometimes spelled) *gunnel*.

HARDTACK: A hard, unsalted bread roll made with flour and water; the utilitarian food of pirates and other sailors. Also called *sea biscuits*.

HELM: The steering wheel of a ship, which controls the rudder and thus the vessel's direction; or the act of manning such a wheel.

HOLD: The lowest chambers in the interior of the hull. Used for storing cargo, prisoners, leakage, and the ship's population of rats.

HULL: The body of a ship built out of wood around the keel. This is what keeps a pirate from the feeding the sharks.

JACOB'S LADDER: A rope-and-wood ladder used to climb into the rigging on square-rigged ships. Not always the safest thing to climb, especially during storms, attacks, and Kraken visits.

JURY RIG: To replace damaged rigging with whatever you can scrounge, or to apply an improvisational approach to any piratical activity.

KEEL: The large, stout beam along the bottom of the hull, around which the ship is built. If the hull is the vessel's ribcage, the keel is its backbone.

KEELHAUL: The corporal and often capital punishment of tying the offending party to a rope, tossing them overboard, and allowing them to be dragged across the barnacle-crusted keel. Not a peaceful way to go, and hence used more as a threat than an actual sentence.

LEE: Downwind, or the direction in which the wind blows away. Particularly handy in the areas of ship navigation and avoiding fragrant crewmates.

LOG: A diary of sorts used by a crewmember, usually the captain, to record various accounts, anecdotes, and other pertinent information aboard ship.

MAN-O'-WAR: A ship of British design that, quite literally, blows away anything else in the water. If a pirate crew is lucky enough to commandeer one of these, few forces in the Caribbean can stop them; if a man-o'-war comes after your little pirate schooner, run.

MAROON: To drop off a prisoner or other undesirable person on a remote island, the idea being that they never leave. The term comes from *cimarron*, the Spanish word for "untamed."

MATE: Technically, an officer or other ranking crewmember of a ship; casually, a term of fraternity among sailors and pirates, especially when augmented to *matey*.

MATELOT: Not to be confused with mate or matey, matelots are pairs of pirates or other seamen who form a tight bond of friendship and intimacy.

MUSKET: A pirate's rifle of choice. This two-handed long arm is an almost surgical implement of mayhem in the hands of a buccaneer.

MUTINY: The act of seizing control of a ship from its captain. This is never done lightly and is often the result of poor management and decision-making on the part of the powers that be.

PLANK: *See* Gangplank.

PORT AND STARBOARD: Left and right, respectively, when facing forward on a vessel. (There is no "your port" or "my starboard." If you're not facing forward, you are wrong.)

QUADRANT: A navigational device. Like a sextant, a quadrant measures angles, but is best used on nighttime objects like stars.

QUARTERDECK: The elevated half-deck that sits above the main deck toward the aft of the ship. This is usually the site of the helm (and the captain, if he's feeling helpful).

QUARTERMASTER: Unlike a quartermaster on land, the quartermaster on a ship isn't responsible for distributing food and provisions, but for maintaining order and smooth, efficient maintenance of the ship. In other words: the actual captain.

RAIL: Wooden barriers nailed to the top of the gunwale on the perimeter of the main deck. Don't go over it.

RAMSHACKLE: A state of shoddy construction, poor upkeep, and overall shabbiness. A point of perverse pirate pride.

RAPIER: A long, slender sword, often with elaborate and ornate handles, used for thrusting, slashing, and dueling.

RIGGING: All those sails and things up there. Go ask someone who's had a little less rum.

RUM: An alcoholic beverage distilled from molasses or cane juice. It greatly impairs the ability to discern the subtle nuances of all those sails.

SABER: A curved backsword with a heavy hand guard. Its heft and shape can do considerable damage. Best used while boarding another ship, since they can double as an axe in a pinch.

SALMAGUNDI: A makeshift British "recipe" popular among pirates: meat, seafood, vegetables fruits, roots, nuts, leaves, flowers, oils, vinegars, sauces—just throw in what you've got.

SCHOONER: A vessel characterized by fore-and-aft sails on two or more masts. Known for both speed and cargo-hauling capability, they are greatly favored by pirates.

SCUPPER: Holes built into ships at deck level that allow seawater and rainwater to drain away. Oh, and sometimes blood.

SCURVY: A malady during which the gums swell and the teeth fall out. Should be prevented by consuming citrus fruits, which abound in the Caribbean.

SCUTTLE: To deliberately sink a ship, usually by putting holes in the hull with axes or cannons. A good way to dispose of the evidence.

SEA LEGS: The state of divine grace attained when a landlubber at sea stops hurling his innards into said sea.

SEXTANT: A handheld navigation device that measures the angle between two objects—particularly the sun and the horizon. Helpful when following your nose doesn't work.

SLOOP: A ship with three or fewer masts and outfitted with up to a dozen guns. Small yet deadly.

SOUNDING LINE: A considerable length of rope, marked in fathoms and fractions thereof, used for measuring the ocean depth. Particularly useful for gauging whether it's safe to temporarily jettison valuable contraband.

SPANISH MAIN: The American mainland surrounding the Gulf of Mexico, and the most fertile source of trans-Caribbean plunder.

SPYGLASS: A small, handheld telescope, usually collapsible, essential for surveying the horizon, faraway ships, and other such oncoming perils or opportunities.

STERN: The area at the very aft of any ship; the opposite of the bow.

STINK POT: A small container or sack stuffed with brimstone and even rotten animal matter, set afire as a weapon to smoke out anyone below decks on a ship under attack.

SWAB: Generally, a mop; more specifically, the mop used to do the mopping; most specifically, the poor wretch who has to use the mop to the do the mopping.

SWIVEL GUN: A cannon mounted on a swiveling base. Good for aiming; bad for a captain if he's got mutineers on board.

TACK: Setting sails at an angle to the wind in order to harness less than optimal atmospheric conditions.

TACKLE: A system of weights and pulleys used for everything from hoisting sails to moving heavy objects, such as treasure chests, from one part of the deck to another.